RECENT RESEARCHES IN THE MUSIC OF THE RENAISSANCE • VOLUME XL

FLORENTINE FESTIVAL MUSIC
1480–1520

Edited by Joseph J. Gallucci, Jr.

A-R EDITIONS, INC. • MADISON

Copyright © 1981, A-R Editions, Inc.

ISSN 0486-123X

ISBN 0-89579-161-7

Library of Congress Cataloging in Publication Data:
Main entry under title:
Florentine festival music 1480-1520.

   (Recent researches in the music of the
Renaissance , ISSN 0486-123X ; v. 40)
    1. Part-songs, Italian.   2. Festivals–Italy–Florence–
Songs and music.   3. Vocal music–Italy–
Florence.   I. Gallucci, Joseph J.   II. Title.
III. Series: Recent researches in the music of the
Renaissance ; v. 40.
M2.R2384   vol. 40   [M1579]   81-17637
ISBN 0-89579-161-7   AACR2

Contents

Preface	vii
Text Synopses	xxii
[1.] "Ben venga maggio"	1
[2.] Canto dei sarti	2
[3.] Canto de' profumieri	4
[4.] Trionfo di Bacco	6
[5.] Canto del mòro di Granata	8
[6.] Canto de' cardoni	10
[7.] Trionfo del vaglio	12
[8.] Trionfo della dea Minerva	14
[9.] Canto de' diavoli	16
[10.] Carro della morte	18
[11.] Trionfo dell'età	20
[12.] Trionfo della compagnia del Broncone	23
[13.] Canto delle dèe [Heinrich] Isa[a]c	26
[14.] Trionfo d'amore e gelosia	28
[15.] Canto di cacciatori	31
[16.] Canto di cacciatori che erano pastori e ninfe	33
[17.] Canto dei capi tondi	36
[18.] Trionfo di diavoli M. Alexander Coppinus [Alessandro Coppini]	39
[19.] Canto de' disamorati	41
[20.] Canto di dominatori	43
[21.] Canto di donne maestre di far cacio	46
[22.] Canto di fanciulle in casa	49
[23.] Canto della fortuna	52

[24.]	Canto dei giudei M. Alexander Coppinus [Alessandro Coppini]	54
[25.]	Canto delle ninfe	57
[26.]	Canto delle parete	60
[27.]	Canto di pastori bacchiatori di bassette Baccio Florentino [Bartolomeo Florentino]	63
[28.]	Canto di pescatori a lenza	66
[29.]	Canto della pomata	68
[30.]	Canto dei poveri che accattano per carità	71
[31.]	Canto della prudenza	73
[32.]	Trionfo della prudenza	75
[33.]	Trionfo dei quattro tempi dell'anno	77
[34.]	Canto dei romiti	80
[35.]	Canto de' savi	83
[36.]	Trionfo delle tre parche	85
[37.]	Canto di uccellatori alle starne Alex. Coppinus [Alessandro Coppini]	88
[38.]	Canto di uomini vecchi allegri e goditori	91
[39.]	Canto di zingane Alex. Coppinus [Alessandro Coppini]	94
[40.]	"Guardate al cielo, el ciel creò costei"	96
[41.]	Canto di lanzi pellegrini	99
[42.]	Canto di lanzi sonatori di rubechine	101
[43.]	Canto di lanzi venturieri	103

Preface

The Composers

For the forty-three festival pieces comprising this edition, composers of the music have been identified by attribution in the source manuscripts for only six. The *Canto delle dèe* (no. 13) is by Heinrich Isaac. The *Canto di pastori bacchiatori di bassette* (no. 27) is by Bartolomeo Florentino. And four other pieces are by Alessandro Coppini: the *Trionfo di diavoli* (no. 18), the *Canto dei giudei* (no. 24), the *Canto di uccellatori alle starne* (no. 37), and the *Canto di zingane* (no. 39).

Isaac, named as the composer of the *Canto delle dèe* in the source manuscript Magliabechiano XIX.141, is too well known to require biographical information in this brief Preface. However, we should mention that Anton Francesco Grazzini, who published the first large collection of texts of festival pieces in the mid-sixteenth century, claimed that Isaac had collaborated with Lorenzo de' Medici on *canti carnascialeschi* and had made a three-voice setting of Lorenzo's *Canto de' confortini*.[1] Unfortunately, the music for this *canto* has not been preserved.

Bartolomeo (Bartolomeo di Michelangelo, Baccio Florentino, Baccio degli Organi, etc.) was born in 1477 and began his professional career as an organist at the age of eleven. He was organist at the principal churches in Florence, and he composed sacred music as well as *ballate* and *canti carnascialeschi*. Bartolomeo is named in manuscript Magliabechiano XIX.117 as the composer of no. 27, the *Canto di pastori bacchiatori di bassette*. He died in 1539.[2]

Alessandro Coppini was born ca. 1465. He was a priest of the Servite order and chaplain at the Hospital of Santa Maria Nuova in Florence. He was also organist at the Hospital and the Church of San Lorenzo. A teacher of singing, he is listed among the Papal Singers in Rome in 1522. He is named as the composer of nos. 18, 24, 37, and 39 in their primary source, manuscript Magliabechiano XIX.141. Apparently he died in Florence in 1527.[3]

The Music

Historical and Cultural Background

Since so few of the composers of this music are identifiable, and of them only Isaac can be considered well known, it is necessary to place this music in its historical and cultural framework. Anyone who has studied the Italian Renaissance has been impressed again and again by the unique relationship between sacred and secular elements prevailing at that time, and some understanding of this relationship is necessary in order to view the music in proper perspective.

The Renaissance, as an outgrowth of fifteenth-century humanism, was essentially a process of secularization. However, while man in all of his humanity was glorified, this was often done (and, to us, surprisingly) within the context of a deeply felt religiosity. The secular was raised to approach the level of the sacred, until a point of perfect equilibrium was reached. Thus, composers used the same basic techniques, imitative and chordal, in both sacred and secular music of all types. Moreover, the same music was frequently used to set both sacred (*lauda*) and secular (*canto* or *trionfo*) texts. This sacred/secular equilibrium is expressed analogously in the visual arts of this period; for example, Botticelli used the same facial features to depict both the Blessed Virgin Mary and Venus, the Goddess of Love.

The music in this edition was composed and performed in Florence, the quintessential center of Italian humanism during the Renaissance. While the Florentines were most industrious in their daily routine of work, they were also perfectly suited temperamentally for occasional public celebrations and revelry. During this period, there were three times set aside each year for elaborate outdoor festivals, and this edition contains examples of music used for each of these occasions.

In the Florentine Renaissance, the carnival season, celebrated in all Christian countries just before the beginning of Lent, culminated as usual in a grand celebration on Shrove Tuesday. The songs performed at this time, *canti carnascialeschi*, were sung by individuals wearing masks and disguises representing the various artisans and tradesmen of the city. The texts were addressed to the women bystanders, and while the songs extolled the merits of the occupation being discussed, they also advertised in coarse double-entendre certain other abilities of which the singers were very proud (see the section Text Synopses, below). The *canti dei lanzi*, with texts mocking the excesses of the German mer-

vii

cenary troops in the service of the Emperor Maximilian, are a subgroup of *canti carnascialeschi*.

The *calendimaggio*, or first day of May, was a celebration in honor of springtime, and it is natural that songs praising youth, love, and spring would play a prominent part in these festivities. Unfortunately, the music for very few of the *canti di maggio* has been preserved, and there is only one such piece in this edition (see no. 1); however, the texts for pieces of this type are found in many fifteenth-century literary anthologies.

The San Giovanni celebrations on June 24, in honor of the patron saint of Florence, date from the early centuries of the Christian era when the city was placed under St. John's protection. Historical evidence indicates that the most elaborate spectacles of the year, the *trionfi*, were used as part of the San Giovanni festivities. In another characteristic Renaissance blending of sacred and secular, these *trionfi* represented events not from the life of the saint, but from ancient history and mythology. The *trionfi* occasionally included short dramatic scenes presented on wagons that traveled throughout the city. Songs similar in musical style to the *canti carnascialeschi* were used for the *trionfi*, although the texts for the two types of pieces usually differ greatly in metric structure and subject matter (see Festival Music from after 1500 and Text Synopses, below).

Thus, each of the three festivals had music that was specifically associated with it. However, there are also instances where the categories of "canto" and "trionfo" are not so clearly defined. For example, no. 10 of this edition (*Carro della morte*) has neither "trionfo" nor "canto" in its title. Another instance of such ambiguity in titles is the *Canto delle dèe* (no. 13), whose mythological subject matter seems more suited to a piece with "trionfo" in its title. Indeed, the choice of terminology in the title is really unimportant. The anthologists were frequently inconsistent in this regard.

Lorenzo de' Medici is often given credit for originating the Florentine festival celebrations, but historical evidence proves that the practice began long before his time. He is a very important figure in the history of the festivals, however, because he composed texts for both *canti carnascialeschi* and *trionfi*, and thereby encouraged other authors in his circle to devote their creativity to these genres. He also expanded the spectacular element of the celebrations by calling on the most skilled artists and craftsmen of the city to provide designs and costumes for the *trionfi*. Lorenzo's well-known desire to acquire linguistic respectability for the Italian vernacular is clearly evidenced by the increasing sophistication of both the subject matter and metric structure of the texts.

Most of the surviving musical settings of *canti carnascialeschi* and *trionfi* are anonymous and are found in one principal manuscript source, Manuscript Magliabechiano XIX.141, in the Biblioteca Nazionale Centrale, Florence. Since this manuscript contains settings of some of Lorenzo's texts, scholars had assumed that all of the extant *canti* and *trionfi* date from Lorenzo's time. However, stylistic evidence indicates that most of the examples of festival pieces in the manuscript date from well after Lorenzo's death in 1492. In the present edition only the first six pieces can be convincingly dated before 1500; the remaining thirty-seven were composed between 1500 and 1520. Since the stylistic criteria for chronological determination concern both text and music, a brief comparison of the characteristics of pre-1500 and post-1500 *canti carnascialeschi* and *trionfi* will follow.

Festival Music from before 1500

The *canti carnascialeschi* and *trionfi* texts from the late fifteenth century are virtually all refrain-(*ripresa*-) stanza forms derived from the *ballata*, having a two- or four-verse refrain and a six- or eight-verse stanza. (Here, and throughout the Preface, "verse" is used according to its definition as one line of poetry.) Most texts have the eight-syllable trochaic verse associated with Italian poetry of the most popular (unlearned) type. None of these texts exhibits the seven- and eleven-syllable combination of iambic verses that had been commonly used in the refined tradition of Italian poetry since the late thirteenth century.

Clearly, however, experimentation with new verse forms for *canti* and *trionfi* was taking place even in the fifteenth century. For example, the May song of the present edition (no. 1) has iambic verses of seven syllables that are in perfect accord with its tone, which is much gentler than that of the *canti carnascialeschi*. The *Canto del mòro di Granata* (no. 5) uses all eleven-syllable verses in the *ottava rima* characteristic of the *strambotto*; this is the only work in the edition to have this poetic form (see Critical Notes). The *Canto de' cardoni* (no. 6) uses all eleven-syllable verses in the compressed *ballata* form, having a two-verse refrain (*ripresa*) and a four-verse stanza. This last-named pattern is found in some of the texts by Lorenzo de' Medici, and reflects his desire to improve the literary quality and sophistication of Italian poetry current in his day.

The musical style of these pre-1500 *canti* and *trionfi* (nos. 1–6) is basically homophonic. The three (occasionally four) voices are equally active, and phraseology is very clear, with a cadence of some type occurring at the end of each verse of text. The composers took great care to insure the proper accentuation of the text, because the words had to be heard above the commotion of an outdoor festival. The simplicity of the musical lines and other features just mentioned indicate that an all-vocal performance, perhaps with one singer to each part, was intended; there is good evidence that not all of those who appeared in costume actually sang. This "choral" texture differentiates the *canti* and *trionfi* from music of the *frottola* type, which seems to have been composed most often for a vocal soloist with instrumental accompaniment. *Canti* and *trionfi* are further distinguished from *frottole* by elements of through-composition; in the great majority of *canti* and *trionfi*, none of the refrain music is repeated in the setting of the stanzas.

Festival Music from after 1500

The sixteenth-century *canti* and *trionfi* (nos. 7–40) often show the seven- and eleven-syllable combination of verses as well as the stanzaic forms without refrain. The historical and mythological subject matter of the *trionfi* did not require a recurrent "main theme" (in the textual sense) as did the *canti carnascialeschi*, in which the principal description of the trade or occupation could be appropriately repeated after the amplification provided in each stanza. The tendency toward strophic through-composition seen in the earlier music is even more obviously present in the post-1500 pieces. Often the entire stanza is set without any musical repetition whatever.

Musically, the homophonic character, clear phraseology, careful accentuation of text, and equal activity of voices (usually four) in these pieces indicate, again, an all-vocal, outdoor performance. However, the post-1500 pieces show some stylistic features not found in the pre-1500 examples.

First, in the middle of many of these pieces, the number of voices is reduced from the usual four to two for a verse or two of text. In these sections, which give additional evidence for an all-vocal conception in that both voices are texted, fragmentary imitation occurs, resulting in a typical contrapuntal duet texture. Second, all of these *trionfi* and *canti carnascialeschi* begin in duple meter, but have at least one sesquialtera (proportionally related triple) section. Moreover, even in the duple-meter portions, the rhythmic-metric organization often is definitely in groupings of three beats, providing a fair amount of metric complexity for pieces that seem at first glance to be so simple. Third, these post-1500 works evidence a strong harmonic organization that is a logical consequence of homophonic conception. A deceptively modern major-minor sound is often present, although many indications of Mixolydian and Dorian modality remain. Fourth, these pieces have a harmonic vocabulary and rich combination of dissonances that are an entirely appropriate musical counterpart to the sophistication of the textual expression.

Taking all of these characteristics into account, one can observe in the festival music a definite presaging of the early Italian madrigal. When, under manneristic influences occurring after 1520, the concern for proper textual accentuation led to the desire for musical interpretation of the text, the older strophic structure had to be abandoned. Thus, it seems more than coincidental that the musical activities of all three of the important early madrigalists—Festa, Verdelot, and Arcadelt—can be traced to Florence.

It need only be added that the differences of textual structure observed in the post-1500 pieces (seven- and eleven-syllable combinations, non-refrain forms, etc.) are not absolutely unequivocal chronological determinants, because even after 1500 composers occasionally returned to the older structural forms if the nature of the subject matter suggested doing so. The clearest examples of this practice are the *canti dei lanzi* (nos. 41–43), songs that mock the German mercenary troops in the service of the Emperor Maximilian. From the standpoint of musical style, the *canti dei lanzi* must be placed in the post-1500 category; yet textually they exhibit some rather archaic features. All are refrain-stanza forms, all have eight-syllable trochaic verses (set appropriately by a much greater use of triple meter than is found in the other festival music), and all have much more musical repetition than other *canti* and *trionfi*. These final works of the edition exhibit the characteristics of these truly popular counterparts to the sophistication of the historical and mythological *trionfi*. Indeed, the *canti dei lanzi* recall characteristics of the old Florentine carnival before Italy was devastated by foreign invaders, and they bring back more than a trace of the carefree atmosphere of Florence in the golden age of Lorenzo the Magnificent.

Sources

Thirty-six of the pieces in this edition (nos. 5, 7, 8, 9, 11–21, and 23–43) have the Manuscript Magliabechiano XIX.141 as their primary source. This manuscript (known also as MS Banco Rari 230) is the most important source of Florentine festival music, and it is now found in the Biblioteca Nazionale Centrale,

Florence (see Plates I and II). The codex was discovered ca. 1850 in the Biblioteca Magliabechiana in Florence, where it had remained uncatalogued among the collection that probably belonged to Antonio Magliabechi (1633–1714). The results of the first attempt at a complete inventory of the manuscript were published in 1939;[4] modern scholarship has clarified and updated much of that information.[5]

Manuscript Magliabechiano XIX.141 contains *frottole* and *strambotti* by such composers as Cara and Tromboncino; so-called *canzoni a ballo* (*ballate*) by Agricola, Isaac, Bartolomeo, and Coppini; *villote* without composer-attributions; and a large number of *canti carnascialeschi* and *trionfi*.[6] Most of the festival pieces in this source seem to have come from the first two decades of the sixteenth century. However, at the end of the manuscript there are earlier examples of the genre; indeed, the final portion of the manuscript seems to contain the oldest music in the entire codex. The three-voice compositions found there (many of which are incomplete) are the only pieces in MS Magl. XIX.141 that can be assumed to have come from the carnival activity during the age of Lorenzo de' Medici. MS Magl. XIX.141 is also an incomplete concordant source for two other pieces (nos. 3 and 4) in the present edition.

Manuscript Magliabechiano XIX.121, also in the Biblioteca Nazionale Centrale and a concordant source for nos. 9 and 41 of this edition, has compositions of widely varying character within its thirty-eight folios. It contains French chansons by Isaac and Hayne (both composers are unidentified in the manuscript), along with pieces showing a Franco-Spanish mixture of text. Also present there are *frottole*, *canti carnascialeschi*, and the only extant versions of some *canti dei lanzi*. Although some of the works in MS Magl. XIX.121 have concordances in MS G.20 in the Biblioteca Comunale, Perugia, notational comparisons indicate that the Florentine source is the later of the two.

The Perugia manuscript, the source for no. 2 in this edition, contains both sacred and secular music of the fifteenth century. In this source hymns, psalms, Magnificats, parts of the Mass, and *laude* are joined with chansons, *frottole*, and four *canti carnascialeschi*. Although the names of a few composers appear in MS G.20 (e.g., Busnois and Urede), none of them can be definitely associated with musical activity in Florence.

Manuscript Banco Rari 337 in the Biblioteca Nazionale Centrale is a single bass partbook that seems to have been compiled somewhat later than MS Magl. XIX.141. This partbook contains no pieces that are concordant with the earliest festival pieces found at the end of MS Magl. XIX.141 (see above), but thirty-nine works from MS Banco Rari 337 are concordant with pieces from the sixteenth-century repertory of MS XIX.141.[7] MS Banco Rari 337 is an important concordance relative to the present edition; it contains bass parts for nos. 10, 11, 13, 14, 16, 22, 24–27, 33, 37, 38, 41, and 43.

A printed anthology of *laude* settings (*Libro primo delle laudi spirituali*) collected by Razzi[8] contains sacred texts that are underlaid to the music originally composed as *canti* and *trionfi*. As is often the case with *laude* based on secular pieces, even the sacred texts are modeled on the textual structure of their sources, a factor that aids greatly in identifying the original secular texts. In Razzi's anthology, there are five pieces whose music is concordant with works in MS Magl. XIX.141 and five that are concordant with pieces in MS Banco Rari 337;[9] one additional concordance is with MS Magl. XIX.121. This indicates not only that the music contained in Razzi's 1563 anthology spans a great number of years; it shows likewise that some of the early *cinquecento* festival music remained popular in one guise or another until well past the middle of the century. Razzi's *Libro primo* is the primary source for the music of nos. 1, 3, 4, 10, and 22 in the present edition; it provides concordances for nos. 8, 13, and 27. The original (secular) texts of these pieces are supplied for this edition from other text sources (see below).

Manuscript Basevi 2440 in the Biblioteca del Conservatorio, Florence, is the only source for no. 6. The manuscript contains 200 pages (in modern pagination) of secular music by such composers as Alessandro Coppini, Bartolomeo Florentino, Heinrich Isaac, and Bernardo Pisano. It is a principal source of Florentine music of the Renaissance.

Manuscript Magliabechiano XIX.117 in the Biblioteca Nazionale Centrale, Florence, is a concordance for no. 27; this is the only piece in the edition that is common to both this manuscript and to MS Magl. XIX.141. The presence of the name "Baccio Florentino" in the MS Magl. XIX.117 version of this piece is the basis for the attribution to Bartolomeo in the present edition.

Editorial Methods

Of the approximately 100 pieces of Florentine festival music composed between 1480 and 1520 that have been preserved in complete versions, the forty-three included in this edition give examples of both "early" and "late" works as well as representative selections of each genre of festival music. Each piece in the edition has been taken from the most complete musical source available. The Critical Notes entry for each piece lists both the primary source and any concordances. Significant variants among sources are documented in the Critical Notes; but variants of a purely graphic nature (which would not change the musical result in any way) are not cited.

As noted above, some of the pieces in this edition have separate sources for music and text. In these works, the primary source of the music either had no underlaid text at all or had a *lauda* text substituted for the original text sometime after the composition was written (see the discussion of Razzi's printed anthology of *laude* on p. x). In such cases, the editor has restored the original text to the music, using a separate text source. Both a text source and a music source are cited in the Critical Notes for these pieces as follows: "Sources containing text only" refers to those manuscripts and prints that contain text without music; the citations of such sources are taken from the listings of *canti* and *trionfi* texts in the anthology edited by Charles S. Singleton.[10] No attempt has been made to record textual variants, but the amount of text present in all musical sources is indicated in the Critical Notes. The majority of transcriptions in the edition gives text and music from the same source. For all pieces obvious textual mistakes are corrected in the transcriptions and cited in the Critical Notes. Archaic spellings (such as "nuj" for "nui") and orthography are replaced by the more modern version, in the interest of greater intelligibility. In certain instances, the editor has had to add letters to the Italian words not only to correct the spelling, but also to complete the syllabification for the appropriate rhythm in the text underlay (see, for example, no. 42, m. 12 of the soprano part, where an e is added to the word "sonar[e]"). Wherever a letter has been editorially added to a word, or when words not found in the source have been editorially supplied, square brackets surround the addition. Sources often omit text where textual repetition is merely suggested by a melisma in the music. Where the text for an entire vocal part of a composition is enclosed in square brackets, it means that this text (usually with the exception of a verse or two) is not underlaid for that particular voice in the source.

Titles are not given for any of the pieces in the manuscript sources for the music. However, the texts of many of these *canti* and *trionfi* were gathered into several printed anthologies (see below, Printed Sources of Texts), where titles were assigned to them, and these titles are used in the present edition wherever they apply. For pieces whose texts have remained unnamed, titles have been formed for this edition from the first line of text; these titles appear within quotation marks.

Ligatures are indicated by solid horizontal brackets above the affected notes; coloration is shown by broken horizontal brackets. All accidentals not present in the source are placed above the staff, according to standard editorial policy.

The mensuration signs given in the sources have been realized here as modern time signatures. The time signature $\frac{3}{2}$ has been consistently used to indicate a measure that has the equivalent of three half-notes, however these notes are subdivided. The designation $\frac{3}{2}$ above the soprano staff indicates triple organization within duple mensuration and, therefore, has a different significance from a change of meter involving the sesquialtera proportional relationship. In the latter case, the nature of the proportion is indicated by an equation that defines the temporal relationship between sections in triple and duple meter; the note given after the "equals sign" (the new section) is to be performed in the same time as that of the note given before the "equals sign" (the old section). The numeral "3" often occurs in the sources at such places (see Plates I and II), and in this edition, this sign is realized as $[\frac{3}{2}]$.

Barlines have been added in accord with the editor's view of the metric structure of the music and the proper accentuation of the text. Needless to say, in music of this period there is often more than one barring that is musically acceptable. Therefore, the barring in each piece is only one of the possible versions. In the refrain- (*ripresa*-) stanza compositions, the refrain is always given first, and is set off from the stanza by two thin barlines.

In two pieces (nos. 4 and 38) the sources indicate repetition simply by stating the first note or two of the section to be repeated. In the edition, this repetition is indicated by means of the instruction "D.S. al Fine."

At times, the sources supply fermate to only the soprano line, although they are clearly intended to apply to all voice parts. When fermate have been added to the edition for the sake of consistency among all of the vocal lines, these fermate are placed in brackets.

Critical Notes

In the Critical Notes, pitches are given as follows: upper-case letters (C) refer to the octave beginning two octaves below middle-c; lower-case letters (c) refer to the octave beginning one octave below middle-c; lower-case letters with single prime (c') refer to the octave beginning with middle-c; and lower-case letters with double prime (c'') refer to the octave beginning one octave above middle-c. All citations of musical variants are made in terms of the reduced time-values used in the transcriptions.

The following sigla, also used in the citations in the Critical Notes, indicate manuscript and printed sources of text and music. The sigla for textual sources are taken from Singleton's publication.

Manuscript Sources of Texts

Sigla	Source Descriptions
L2	Florence: Biblioteca Laurenziana, MS Laurenziano-Ashburnhamiano 606.
M4	Florence: Biblioteca Nazionale Centrale, MS Magliabechiano II.II.226.
M6	Florence: Biblioteca Nazionale Centrale, MS Magliabechiano II.IV.252 (VII.343).
M12	Florence: Biblioteca Nazionale Centrale, MS Magliabechiano VII.735.
Mk	Lucca: Biblioteca Governativa, MS Moucke 27 (MS 1512).
P1	Florence: Biblioteca Nazionale Centrale, MS Palatino 67.
P2	Florence: Biblioteca Nazionale Centrale, MS Palatino 173.
P4	Florence: Biblioteca Nazionale Centrale, MS Palatino 288.
Panc.1	Florence: Biblioteca Nazionale Centrale, MS Panciatichiano 25.
R2	Florence: Biblioteca Riccardiana, MS Riccardiano 2731.

Printed Sources of Texts

Sigla	Source Descriptions
I	*Canzone per andare in maschera per carnesciale facte da più persone.* [Florence: Bartolomeo de' Libri?, ca. 1494.]
II	*Canzone per andare in maschera per carnesciale facte da più persone.* [Florence: Lorenzo Morgiani and Giovanni Petri?, ca. 1494.]
VI	*Canzona della morte. Canzona del bronchone. Canzona del diamante & della chazuola.* [No city, printer, or date; not before 1513.]
VII	*La canzona de morti.* [No city, printer, or date; not before 1512.]
IX	*Tutti i trionfi, carri, mascheeate* [sic] *ò canti carnascialeschi....* Collected and edited by Anton Francesco Grazzini (called *il Lasca*). Florence: [Lorenzo Torrentino], 1559.
X	*Canzoni, o vero mascherate carnascialesche di M. Gio. Battista dell'Ottonaio....* Florence: Lorenzo Torrentino, 1560.
XI	*Tutti i trionfi, carri, mascherate ò canti carnascialeschi....* Edited and enlarged by Rinaldo Maria Bracci [known also as Neri del Boccia and Decio Laberio], 2 vols., 2d ed. [Lucca: Filippo Maria Benedini], 1750.

Manuscript Sources of Music

Sigla	Source Descriptions
G.20	Perugia: Biblioteca Comunale, MS G.20.
117	Florence: Biblioteca Nazionale Centrale, MS Magliabechiano XIX.117.
121	Florence: Biblioteca Nazionale Centrale, MS Magliabechiano XIX.121.
141	Florence: Biblioteca Nazionale Centrale, MS Magliabechiano XIX.141 (known also as MS Banco Rari 230).
337	Florence: Biblioteca Nazionale Centrale, MS Banco Rari 337 (a single bass partbook).
2440	Florence: Biblioteca del Conservatorio, MS Basevi 2440.

Printed Sources of Music

Siglum	Source Description
Lib. I°	*Libro primo delle laudi spirituali da diversi eccell. e divoti autori, antiche e moderni composte....* Collected and edited by Serafino Razzi. Venice: At the request of the Giunti of Florence, 1563.

Additional information on these sources as well as further documentary and stylistic evidence affirming the citations and assertions in the following Critical Notes can be found in the editor's dissertation.[11]

[1.] "Ben venga maggio"

Author of text: Angelo Poliziano.
Source of music: *Libro primo delle laudi spirituali...*, fol. 15v ("Ecco 'l Messia, ecco 'l Messia").
Transcription of music according to *Lib. I°*.
Text taken from Giosuè Carducci, *Le Stanze, l'Orfeo e le rime, di Messer Angelo Ambrogini Poliziano* (Florence, 1863), pp. 295-297.

M. 1, soprano is labeled "altus," and alto is labeled "cantus." The text of the *lauda* "Ecco 'l Messia, ecco 'l Messia" is by Lucrezia de' Medici, the Magnifico's mother, who died in 1482. The text was published in a collection of *laude* dated 1485 (1486 N.S.) with the indication that the music of "Ben venga maggio" was to be used in setting Lucrezia's text. It happens often that the music of a secular piece can be reconstructed only by discovering a *lauda* based upon it and resubstituting the original secular text.

Razzi also published a two-voice piece with a slightly different title ("Ecco, ecco 'l Messia") on fol. 16 of *Lib. I°*, the music of which is unrelated to the piece given in our transcription. Five additional *lauda* texts, all to be sung to the music of "Ecco 'l Messia," are included in his publication: "Ecco la stella, ecco la stella" by Razzi (fols. 16v–17); "Ecco 'l diletto, ecco 'l diletto" by Razzi (fol. 17); "Suso a Maria, suso a Maria" by Razzi (fols. 17–17v); "Con humil core, con humil core" by Feo Belcari (fol. 17v); and "Ecco 'l Signore, ecco 'l Signore" by "authore incerto" (fols. 17v–18).

[2.] Canto dei sarti

Source of music: MS Perugia G.20, fol. 116.
Sources containing text only: I; II.

Transcription of music according to MS G.20. Text taken from MS G.20.

M. 16, alto, note 2 is d'.

[3.] Canto de' profumieri

Author of text: Lorenzo de' Medici.
Sources of music: *Libro primo delle laudi spirituali . . .* , fols. 64v [68v]–69 ("O maligno e duro core" [Lorenzo de' Medici]); MS Magl. XIX.141 (soprano only), fol. 144v.
Sources containing text only: R2; I; II; IX (attributed to Jacopo da Bientina in R2 and IX).

Transcription of music according to *Lib. I°*. Text taken from MS Magl. XIX.141.

M. 11, soprano, text for note 1 is *cia* in MS 141. M. 37, soprano, rhythm for this m. is whole-note followed by half-note in MS 141. M. 43, soprano, rhythm for first 3 beats is half-note followed by quarter-note (g', g') in MS 141. Lorenzo's *lauda* text "O maligno e duro core" appeared in a collection believed to have been published in 1489. The indication is given that the music of the *Canto de' valenziani* is to be used in setting this *lauda*. The *Canto de' valenziani* and the *Canto de' profumieri* are identical, as the first verse of the refrain shows.

[4.] Trionfo di Bacco

Author of text: Lorenzo de' Medici.
Sources of music: *Libro primo delle laudi spirituali . . .* , fols. 10v–11 ("Quant'è grande la bellezza"); MS Magl. XIX.141 (tenor and bass only, untexted), fol. 150.
Sources containing text only: R2; I; II; IX.

Transcription of music according to *Lib. I°*. Text taken from *Lorenzo de' Medici il Magnifico: Tutte le opere*, ed. Gigi Cavalli (Milan, 1958), I:153–154.

M. 8, tenor and bass, notes 1 and 2, rhythm is whole-note in MS 141; rhythm of notes 3 and 4 is dotted half and quarter in MS 141. M. 13, tenor, note 1 is repeated in MS 141; bass, note 1 is repeated in MS 141. M. 14, tenor, note 1 is f' in MS 141. M. 17, bass, notes 3 and 4 are dotted quarter and eighth in MS 141. M. 19, tenor, notes 4 and 5 replaced by half-note (b) in MS 141. M. 20, tenor, notes 1 and 2 replaced by whole-note (c') in MS 141. M. 23, soprano, note 3 is c" in *Lib. I°*. M. 27, tenor, notes 4–5 replaced by a half-note (f') in MS 141. M. 28, tenor, notes 1–2 replaced by a whole-note (g') in MS 141. M. 35, bass, note 1 replaced by 2 quarter-notes (d, d) in MS 141. M. 36, bass, notes 1–2 replaced by a whole-note (d) in MS 141. M. 38, bass, notes 3–4 replaced by a dotted half-note (c) in MS 141. M. 39, tenor, notes 1–2 replaced by a whole-note (g) in MS 141.

The collection of *lauda* texts of 1489 contains "Quant'è grande la bellezza" and gives Lorenzo de' Medici as the author. The print has instructions that this *lauda* is to be sung to the music of Lorenzo's *Canto delle forese*. However, the *lauda* shows such unmistakable signs of having been modeled on Lorenzo's *Trionfo di Bacco* that a convincing suggestion can be made that the music of the *lauda* originally set the *Trionfo di Bacco* rather than the *Canto delle forese*. It is a characteristic of *lauda* texts that the opening verse in particular is structurally very similar to the parent secular text.

[5.] Canto del mòro di Granata

Source of music: MS Magl. XIX.141, fols. 143v–144.
Sources containing only text: Panc. 1, R2, IX.

Transcription of music according to MS Magl. XIX.141. Text taken from MS Magl. XIX.141.

M. 30, note 2-m. 34, soprano, text underlay is *disacete* in MS 141.

As mentioned in the Preface, this text uses the eleven-syllable verse quantity and *ottava rima* of the *strambotto*. It remains unique in the literature; the editor has been unable to locate any other fifteenth- or sixteenth-century *canto* or *trionfo* text having this poetic form.

[6.] Canto de' cardoni

Author of text: Lorenzo di Filippo Strozzi.
Source of music: MS Basevi 2440, pp. 86–89.
Sources containing text only: L2; M6; R2; IX.

Transcription of music according to MS 2440. Text taken from MS 2440.

M. 1, bass, notes 2 and 3 doubled with colored notes at the octave above in MS 2440.

This text is mentioned in the Preface as exemplifying late fifteenth-century experimentation with verse forms, since it has all eleven-syllable verses and is written in the compressed *ballata* form. Source L2 indicates that Strozzi composed this text in his youth. Since his date of birth has been established as 1482, it would seem reasonable to date this piece ca. 1495–1500.

[7.] Trionfo del vaglio

Author of text: Fruosino Bonini.
Source of music: MS Magl. XIX.141, fols. 127v–128.
Sources containing text only: M12; R2; IX.

Transcription of music according to MS 141. Text taken from MS 141.

Source M12 gives "Fruosino" as the author of the text of this *trionfo* and 3 February 1505 (1506 N.S.) as its date.

[8.] Trionfo della dea Minerva

Author of text: Agnolo Divizio da Bibbiena.
Sources of music: MS Magl. XIX.141, fols. 115v–116; *Libro primo delle laudi spirituali* . . . , fols. 134v–135.
Sources containing text only: M12; Mk; R2; IX.

Transcription of music according to MS 141. Text taken from MS 141.

M. 6, alto, whole-note has a fermata in *Lib. I°*. M. 7, alto, note 1 omitted in *Lib. I°*. M. 11, soprano and bass, notes 1–2 replaced by a whole-note in *Lib. I°*. Mm. 11–12, tenor, rhythm of these mm. is dotted whole-note (d') and half-note (d') in *Lib. I°*. M. 12, soprano and bass, note 1 replaced by 2 half-notes in *Lib. I°*. M. 13, alto, note 2 omitted in MS 141, but present in *Lib. I°*. M. 18, soprano, note 1 is half-note in *Lib. I°*; tenor, note 2 is d in *Lib. I°*. M. 23, soprano and bass, note 1 replaced by 2 half-notes in *Lib. I°*. M. 25, soprano, notes 1–2 replaced by a whole-note in *Lib. I°*. M. 26, soprano, alto, bass, notes 1–2 replaced by a whole-note in *Lib. I°*. M. 28, soprano, notes 1-2 replaced by whole-note in *Lib. I°*. M. 29, alto and tenor, note 1 replaced by 2 half-notes in *Lib. I°*. M. 33, alto, tenor, bass, note 1 replaced by 2 half-notes in *Lib. I°*. M. 35, alto, notes 2–3 replaced by half-note and tie omitted in *Lib. I°*. M. 36, bass, note 1 replaced by 2 half-notes in *Lib. I°*. M. 37, soprano, only one-half m. of rest here in *Lib. I°*. M. 38, all parts, rhythm for this m. is whole-note followed by half-note in *Lib. I°*.

Source M12 states that this text was composed by Poliziano when the Cardinal [Giovanni] de' Medici received the red hat (1492). The *lauda* text (with identical first verse) was attributed to Lorenzo de' Medici in a collection believed to have been printed in 1510. This collection is the *Laude vecchie e nuove*, printed at the request of Piero Pacini of Pescia. The determination of the date of its printing is by Gustavo Camillo Galletti, who edited a reprint in 1863 (Galletti's publication is titled *Laude spirituali di Feo Belcari, di Lorenzo de' Medici, di Francesco d'Albizzo, di Castellano Castellani e di altri* [Florence, 1863]). On the basis of textual analysis alone, Carducci asserted that Poliziano is probably not the author of the *trionfo* (see *Le Stanze* . . . , pp. 381-382). Indeed, both the textual structure of the *trionfo* and the *lauda* and the musical style indicate composition after 1500. The final stanza of text indicates composition before Cardinal de' Medici ascended to the Papacy (1513). Sources R2 and IX attribute the text to Bibbiena.

[9.] Canto de' diavoli

Author of text: Niccolò Machiavelli
Sources of music: MS Magl. XIX.141, fols. 134v–135; MS Magl. XIX.121, fols. 15v–16.
Sources containing text only: R2; IX.

Transcription of music according to MS 141. Text taken from MS 141.

M. 1, bass, although a bass clef appears at the beginning of this line in MS 121, the notes are written according to the tenor clef. M. 5, alto, note 1 is f' in MS 121. M. 6, alto, note 2 is d' in MS 121. M. 8, soprano, note 1 has colored semibreve instead of breve (♩♮♩♩ instead of ♮♩♩) in MS 121; bass, note 1 has no flat in MS 121. M. 13, tenor, note 1 replaced by half-note (g') followed by quarter-note (g') in MS 121. M. 14, alto, note 1 is f' in MS 121. M. 15, all parts, note 1 is a half-note in MS 121. M. 16, tenor, note 1 is c'. M. 18, alto, note 6 is c', note 7 is b, and there is an extra eighth-note (a) added before note 8 in MS 121. M. 20, alto, notes 1–2 replaced by a whole-note in MS 121. M. 26, soprano and bass, note 1 replaced by 2 half-notes in MS 121. MS 121 does not have the third additional stanza of text. A *lauda* text, "Già fummo eletti, ed or siam riprovati," in the 1510 collection referred to above indicates that it is to be sung to the music of this *canto*.

[10.] Carro della morte

Author of text: Antonio Alamanni.
Sources of music: *Libro primo delle laudi spirituali* . . . , fols. 100v–101 (text attributed to M. Castellano); MS Banco Rari 337 (bass only, untexted), fol. 99v.
Sources containing text only: P1; P2; R2; VII; IX.
Transcription of music according to *Lib. I°*.

M. 2, bass, note 1 is a in *Lib. I°*. Mm. 13–14, alto, rhythm is whole-note instead of double whole-note in *Lib. I°*. Mm. 13–14, bass, tie omitted and fermata added to note 1 of M. 14 in MS 337. M. 25, bass, note 1 (f) is present in MS 337. M. 28, bass, note 1 is d in *Lib. I°*. Mm. 30–31, bass, note 2 is a whole-note followed by a half-note (a) in MS 337. M. 34, bass, note 1 is c in *Lib. I°*. M. 38, alto, note 2 is a whole-note in *Lib. I°*. M. 39, all voices have double whole-notes in this m. in *Lib. I°*; there are 2 whole-notes in MS 337.

Giorgio Vasari, in his "Lives of the Great Artists" published in 1550, gives the opinion that this *Carro* signified the return of the Medici to power in 1512. While the Medici were exiles, they were as dead people, who were to rise again to life shortly. The detailed physical description of the wagon that Vasari gives lends weight to his opinion (see his *Vite de' più eccellenti architetti pittori et scultori italiana da Cimabue insino a' tempi nostri*, II [Milan, 1943]: 51–54). The text seems to have a strongly Savonarolian flavor, but other sources suggest 1506 as the correct date (see Singleton, *Canti carnascialeschi . . .*, pp. 478-479).

[11.] Trionfo dell'età

Author of text: Antonio Alamanni.
Sources of music: MS Magl. XIX.141, fols. 135v–137; MS Banco Rari 337 (bass only, fifth and sixth verses of first stanza only), fol. 64v.
Sources containing text only: Mk; R2; IX.
Transcription of music according to MS 141.

M. 10, note 3–m. 11, note 5, bass, this passage is repeated in MS 141. M. 19, bass, notes 1 and 2 replaced by dotted half-note in MS 337. M. 21, bass, note 2 is a whole-note in MS 337. M. 33, bass, note 1 replaced by 2 half-notes in MS 337. M. 40, bass, note 1 has no flat and notes 4 and 5 are replaced by a dotted half-note in MS 337.

Historians have asserted that this *trionfo* and the following (no. 12) were performed in honor of Cardinal Giovanni de' Medici's election to the Papacy in 1513. Vasari's description of the two *trionfi* (*Le vite . . .*, III [Milan, 1943]: 41-45) shows beyond doubt that they were among the most opulent and extravagant presentations that the city had ever seen. The *Trionfo dell'età* was produced by a group of gentlemen called the Compagnia del Diamante, under the leadership of Giuliano de' Medici, brother of Cardinal Giovanni. It consisted of three lavishly adorned wagons to represent, respectively, Youth, Maturity, and Old Age. The most renowned artisans of the city worked on this *trionfo*, including Jacopo da Pontormo, who painted all three wagons.

[12.] Trionfo della compagnia del Broncone

Author of text: Jacopo Nardi.
Source of music: MS Magl. XIX.141, fols. 88v–89.
Sources containing text only: Mk; Panc. 1; R2; VI; IX.
Transcription of music according to MS 141. Text taken from MS 141.

As explained in the notes to no. 11, this *trionfo* was the second one in honor of Cardinal Giovanni de' Medici's election to the Papacy in 1513. The Compagnia del Broncone was a group of gentlemen under the leadership of Lorenzo de' Medici, grandson of the Magnifico. The *trionfo* was designed by Jacopo Nardi, and consisted of six elaborately decorated wagons representing six golden ages in history and mythology. The first, the age of Saturn and Janus, was followed by the age of Numa Pompilius. Then came the consulate of Titus Manlius Torquatus. The age of Caesar was represented in the fourth wagon, and the fifth wagon followed with the age of Caesar Augustus. Last was shown the age of Trajan. These wagons were accompanied by hundreds of men in lavish costumes appropriate to the principal characteristics of each age. An undated sixteenth-century print gives the date 1512 with the text of this *trionfo*. If the date is correct, and if these celebrations were actually occasioned by the Papacy of Cardinal Giovanni de' Medici, this *trionfo* would have had to take place between 11 March 1512 (O.S.), when news of his election reached Florence, and 25 March, the beginning of the new year.

[13.] Canto delle dèe

Composer of music: Heinrich Isaac.
Sources of music: MS Magl. XIX.141, fols. 116v–117; *Libro primo delle laudi spirituali . . .*, fols. 144v–145 ("Vergine santa, gloriosa, e degna"). MS Banco Rari 337 (bass only, fifth verse of first stanza only), fol. 51v.
Sources containing text only: Mk; R2; XI.
Transcription of music according to MS 141. Text taken from MS 141.

M. 5, soprano, note 1 replaced by 2 half-notes in *Lib. I°*. M. 12, alto, notes 1–2 replaced by whole-note in *Lib. I°*. M. 13, alto, note 1 replaced by 2 half-notes in *Lib. I°*; bass, notes 1–2 replaced by whole-note in MS 337. M. 19, bass, note 1 is a whole-note, and rest is omitted in *Lib. I°*. M. 28, tenor, notes 1-2 replaced by dotted half-note in *Lib. I°*. M. 34, tenor, note 1 replaced by 2 half-notes in *Lib. I°*. M. 39, soprano, notes 1–2 replaced by whole-note in *Lib. I°*. M. 41, bass, note 1 is e-flat in *Lib. I°*. M. 43, bass, note 1 is doubled at the octave below in MS 337.

[14.] Trionfo d'amore e gelosia

Sources of music: MS Magl. XIX.141, fols. 117v–118; MS Banco Rari 337 (bass only, untexted), fol. 54v.

Sources containing text only: M4; Mk; Panc. 1; R2; IX.

Transcription of music according to MS 141. Text taken from MS 141.

M. 6, bass, notes 1–2 replaced by dotted half-note in MS 337. M. 13, tenor, note 5 is possibly an eighth-note in MS 141. M. 36, bass, note 2 is a in MS 141 and in MS 337.

[15.] Canto di cacciatori

Source of music: MS Magl. XIX.141, fols. 94v–95.
Transcription of music according to MS 141. Text taken from MS 141.

M. 47, alto, note 2–m.48, alto has a double whole-note (f') in MS 141.

[16.] Canto di cacciatori che erano pastori e ninfe

Sources of music: MS Magl. XIX.141, fols. 121v–122; MS Banco Rari 337 (bass only, untexted), fol. 61v.

Sources containing text only: Mk; R2; IX.

Transcription of music according to MS 141. Text taken from MS 141.

M. 38, bass, note 1 replaced by 2 half-notes in MS 337. M. 41, bass, note 1 is B-flat in MS 337. The first verse as it appears in manuscript sources other than MS 141 ("Donne, se 'l ciel aspiri ai vostri amori") creates a regular rhyme scheme in the refrain.

[17.] Canto dei capi tondi

Author of text: Giovanni Battista dell' Ottonaio.
Source of music: MS Magl. XIX.141, fols. 82v–84.
Sources containing text only: Mk; R2; IX; X.
Transcription of music according to MS 141. Text taken from MS 141.

M. 11, alto, note 3 is a quarter-note in MS 141. M. 12, alto, notes 1 and 2 are quarter-notes in MS 141.

[18.] Trionfo di diavoli

Composer of music: Alessandro Coppini.
Author of text: Guglielmo detto il Giuggiola.
Source of music: MS Magl. XIX.141, fols. 40v-41.
Sources containing text only: Mk; R2; IX.
Transcription of music according to MS 141. Text taken from MS 141.

[19.] Canto de' disamorati

Source of music: MS Magl. XIX.141, fols. 128v–129.

Sources containing text only: Mk; R2; IX.
Transcription of music according to MS 141. Text taken from MS 141.

[20.] Canto di dominatori

Author of text: Jacopo da Bientina.
Source of music: MS Magl. XIX.141, fols. 99v–100.
Sources containing text only: Mk; R2.
Transcription of music according to MS 141. Text taken from MS 141.

[21.] Canto di donne maestre di far cacio

Author of text: Jacopo da Bientina.
Source of music: MS Magl. XIX.141, fols. 95v–96.
Sources containing text only: P4; Panc. 1; R2; IX.
Transcription of music according to MS 141. Text taken from MS 141.

M. 13, alto, note 3 is written as a minim, but the scribe has crossed out the stem to change it to a semibreve in MS 141. M. 18, alto, note 3 has something pasted over it in MS 141.

[22.] Canto di fanciulle in casa

Author of text: Giovanni Battista dell' Ottonaio.
Sources of music: *Libro primo delle laudi spirituali* . . . , fols. 70v–72. ("Amor che in terra il tuo amor mandasti," text attributed to Fra Angelo Bettini); MS Banco Rari 337 (bass only, first verse of text only), fol. 73v.

Sources containing text only: Mk; R2; IX; X.

Transcription of music according to *Lib. I°*. Text taken from Singleton, *Canti carnascialeschi* . . . , pp. 311-312.

M. 11, soprano and bass, this m. is extraordinary in its dissonance. M. 16, bass, note 1 is a half-note in *Lib. I°*. M. 18, bass, note 3 replaced by 2 quarter-notes in MS 337. M. 31, alto, tenor clef inserted between notes 2 and 3, but pitches continue to be given according to alto clef in *Lib. I°*. M. 32, alto, half-rest inserted after note 1 in *Lib. I°*. M. 37, bass, notes 1–2 replaced by a dotted half-note in MS 337. M. 38, bass, notes 1–2 replaced by a dotted half-note in MS 337.

[23.] Canto della fortuna

Source of music: MS Magl. XIX.141, fols. 129v–130.

Sources containing text only: Mk; R2; XI.

Transcription of music according to MS 141. Text taken from MS 141.

M. 24, bass, note 2 is unclear in MS 141.

[24.] Canto dei giudei

Composer of music: Alessandro Coppini.
Author of text: Giovanni Battista dell' Ottonaio.
Sources of music: MS Magl. XIX.141, fols. 42v-43; MS Banco Rari 337 (bass only, untexted), fol. 90v.
Sources containing text only: Mk; Panc. 1; R2; IX; X.
Transcription of music according to MS 141. Text taken from MS 141.

M. 21, soprano, note 1, text underlay [che], in the source this syllable is at the edge of the page and illegible; alto part no longer has a b-flat in the signature; soprano, from note 3, this part no longer has a b'-flat in the signature in MS 141. Mm. 37-38, bass, notes in these mm. doubled at the octave below in MS 337.

[25.] Canto delle ninfe

Sources of music: MS Magl. XIX.141, fols. 113v-114; MS Banco Rari 337 (bass only, untexted), fol. 58v.
Sources containing text only: Mk; Panc. 1; R2; XI.
Transcription of music according to MS 141. Text taken from MS 141.

M. 1, soprano, text is *tuo* in MS 141. M. 7, tenor, note 1, black note c' added below f' in MS 141. M. 43, bass, note 1, g added below d' in MS 337.

[26.] Canto delle parete

Author of text: Guglielmo detto il Giuggiola.
Sources of music: MS Magl. XIX.141, fols. 119v, 121; MS Banco Rari 337 (bass only, untexted), fol. 62v.
Sources containing text only: Mk; Panc. 1; R2; IX.
Transcription of music according to MS 141. Text taken from MS 141.

M. 16, bass, notes 1-2, rhythm is dotted-quarter and eighth in MS 337 (both notes are colored).

[27.] Canto di pastori bacchiatori di bassette

Composer of music: Bartolomeo Florentino.
Author of text: Jacopo da Bientina.
Sources of music: MS Magl. XIX.141, fols. 133v–134; MS Banco Rari 337 (bass only, first verse of refrain only), fol. 65v; MS Magl. XIX.117 (first verse of refrain only), fols. 17v–18; *Libro primo delle laudi spirituali . . .* , fols. 51v–52 ("Si pensassi a piacer del paradiso," text attributed to Feo Belcari).
Sources containing text only: Mk; Panc. 1; R2; IX.
Transcription of music according to MS 141. Text taken from MS 141.

M. 2, all parts, notes 1–2 replaced by whole-note in *Lib. I°*. M. 4, alto, notes 1–2 replaced by whole-note in MS 117 and *Lib. I°*. M. 5, soprano, notes 1 and 3 are dotted quarters, notes 2 and 4 are eighth-notes in *Lib. I°*. M. 9, soprano and tenor, notes 1–2 replaced by whole-note in *Lib. I°*. M. 10, bass, note 1 replaced by half-note followed by quarter-note in MS 117. M. 13, bass, note 1 is f in *Lib. I°*. M. 14, alto, note 1 replaced by half-note followed by quarter-note in MS 117; bass, notes 1–2 replaced by whole-note in MS 117 and *Lib. I°*. Mm. 15–16, soprano and alto, notes 1–2 replaced by whole-note in each m. in *Lib. I°*. M. 16, tenor, notes 1–2 replaced by whole-note in *Lib. I°*. M. 21, tenor, note 3 is a quarter-note, note 4 is a quarter-note in MS 117. M. 24, alto, note 1 replaced by two half-notes in *Lib. I°*. M. 25, alto, notes 1 and 2 replaced by dotted half-note in *Lib. I°*. M. 26, soprano and bass, notes 1–2 replaced by a whole-note in *Lib. I°*; alto, notes 1 and 2 replaced by a whole-note in MS 117. M. 27, alto, note 2 through note 3 of m. 28 replaced by whole-note (c') followed by half-note (c') in MS 117. M. 28, tenor, notes 2–3 replaced by half-note in MS 117. M. 31, soprano, notes 1–2 replaced by dotted half-note in MS 117 and *Lib. I°*; bass, note 1 replaced by half-note followed by quarter-note in MS 337. M. 32, alto, notes 1–2 replaced by half-note in MS 117. M. 33, alto, note 1 has no flat in MS 117; bass, note 1 has no flat in *Lib. I°*. M. 40, bass, note 2 doubled at octave below with black note in MS 337. M. 41, bass, notes 1 and 2 doubled at octave below with black notes in MS 337; bass, note 1 is a quarter-note in MS 117. M. 47, bass, notes 1–2 replaced by a whole-note in MS 117.

Structural features of the *lauda* published in *Lib. I°* raise questions concerning Razzi's attribution to Feo Belcari, but the consideration of Bartolomeo's dates indicates that Belcari could not have been the composer. Belcari died in 1484, only about ten years after Bartolomeo's birth.

[28.] Canto di pescatori a lenza

Author of text: Guglielmo detto il Giuggiola.
Source of music: MS Magl. XIX.141, fols. 87v–88.
Sources containing text only: R2; IX.
Transcription of music according to MS 141. Text taken from MS 141.

[29.] Canto della pomata

Source of music: MS Magl. XIX.141, fols. 122v–123.
Sources containing text only: R2; IX.
Transcription of music according to MS 141. Text taken from MS 141.

[30.] Canto dei poveri che accattano per carità

Author of text: Lorenzo de' Medici?
Source of music: MS Magl. XIX.141, fols. 105v–106.
Sources containing text only: R2; IX.
Transcription of music according to MS 141. Text taken from MS 141.

M. 19, soprano, notes 3 and 4 are quarter-notes in MS 141; alto, notes 2–4 are unclear in MS 141.

The editors of Lorenzo's poetry claim that this text is "of doubtful authenticity." (See Attilo Simioni, ed., *Lorenzo de' Medici il Magnifico: Opere*, 2 vols. [Bari, 1913-1914].) Therefore, we cannot unequivocally state that Lorenzo is the author, although the use of all seven-syllable verses is more characteristic of fifteenth- than of sixteenth-century *canti*. Stylistic evidence shows that the music unquestionably comes from the sixteenth century, and the placement of the piece in the manuscript further confirms this. This *canto* is not found at the end of the codex with the earliest repertory, but in a fascicle toward the middle. However, the sixteenth-century musical style does not absolutely negate Lorenzo's authorship of the text. In the case of an author as famous as the Magnifico, his texts might well have been reset long after his death to celebrate his memory or to honor one of his descendants.

[31.] Canto della prudenza

Source of music: MS Magl. XIX.141, fols. 132v–133.
Sources containing text only: R2; XI.
Transcription of music according to MS 141. Text taken from MS 141.

[32.] Trionfo della prudenza

Source of music: MS Magl. XIX.141, fols. 131v–132.
Sources containing text only: R2; IX.
Transcription of music according to MS 141. Text taken from MS 141.

[33.] Trionfo dei quattro tempi dell'anno

Sources of music: MS Magl. XIX.141, fols. 114v–115; MS Banco Rari 337 (bass only, untexted), fol. 56v.
Sources containing text only: Mk; Panc. 1; R2; IX.
Transcription of music according to MS 141. Text taken from MS 141.

M. 4, bass, note 1 replaced by half-note followed by quarter-note in MS 337. M. 10, bass, notes 1-2 replaced by dotted half-note in MS 337. M. 18, bass, half-rest replaced by half-note (c) in MS 337. M. 34, bass, note 1 is a whole-note and rest is omitted in MS 337.

[34.] Canto dei romiti

Source of music: MS Magl. XIX.141, fols. 123v–124.
Sources containing text only: Mk; R2; IX.
Transcription of music according to MS 141. Text taken from MS 141.

M. 4, alto and bass, half-rest inserted after note 1 in MS 141. M. 9, alto, note 1 is a whole-note followed by a half-rest in MS 141.

[35.] Canto de' savi

Author of text: Alessandro di Rinaldo Bracci?
Source of music: MS Magl. XIX.141, fols. 130v–131.
Sources containing text only: Mk; R2; XI.
Transcription of music according to MS 141. Text taken from MS 141.

M. 25, bass, notes 1 and 2 doubled at the octave below by black notes in MS 141.

This text is anonymous in all manuscript sources and is not found in Source IX. Rinaldo Bracci attributed it to Alessandro Bracci in Source XI, basing the attribution on the now-lost "Codex Bracci" (see Singleton, *Canti carnascialeschi . . .* , p. 464).

[36.] Trionfo delle tre parche

Author of text: Giovanni Battista dell' Ottonaio?
Source of music: MS Magl. XIX.141, fols. 89v–90.
Sources containing text only: Mk; R2; VI; IX.
Transcription of music according to MS 141. Text taken from MS 141.

M. 27, soprano, note 2 is an eighth-note in MS 141. Source R2 is the only source attributing this text to Ottonaio; all other sources give no attribution.

[37.] Canto di uccellatori alle starne

Composer of music: Alessandro Coppini.
Author of text: Giovan Francesco del Bianco.
Sources of music: MS Magl. XIX.141, fols. 37v–39; MS Banco Rari 337 (bass only, fourth verse of first stanza only), fol. 71v.
Sources containing text only: Mk; R2; IX.
Transcription of music according to MS 141. Text taken from MS 141.

M. 2, bass, notes 2–3 replaced by a half-note in MS 337. M. 21, bass, note 1 has no flat in MS 337.

[38.] Canto di uomini vecchi allegri e goditori

Author of text: Guglielmo detto il Giuggiola?
Sources of music: MS Magl. XIX.141, fols.

126v–127; MS Banco Rari 337 (bass only, untexted), fol. 66v.

Sources containing text only: Mk; Panc. 1; R2; IX.

Transcription of music according to MS 141. Text taken from MS 141.

M. 27, bass, note 1 is a whole-note and rest 1 is omitted in MS 337. Source R2 attributes this text to Giuggiola; all other sources give no attribution.

[39.] Canto di zingane

Composer of music: Alessandro Coppini.
Author of text: Guglielmo detto il Giuggiola.
Source of music: MS Magl. XIX.141, fols. 39v-40.
Transcription of music according to MS 141. Text taken from MS 141.

Mm. 24–27, alto, text is *condotte* in MS 141. M. 27, tenor, one additional m. of rest inserted here in MS 141.

[40.] "Guardate al cielo, el ciel creò costei"

Source of music: MS Magl. XIX.141, fols. 137v–138.

Transcription of music according to MS 141. Text taken from MS 141.

[41.] Canto di lanzi pellegrini

Author of text: Guglielmo detto il Giuggiola.
Sources of music: MS Magl. XIX.141, fols. 138v-139; MS Magl. XIX.121, fols. 11v-12 (the penultimate stanza of text is not present); MS Banco Rari 337 (bass only, untexted), fol. 68v.

Sources containing text only: Mk; R2; IX.

Transcription of music according to MS 141. Text taken from MS 141.

M. 4, bass, notes 1 and 2 are doubled at the octave below in MS 337. Mm. 7 (notes 3–4) and 8, soprano, text is *biugilei* in MS 141. M. 8, soprano, notes 1–2 replaced by whole-note in MS 121; bass, note 1 doubled at octave below in MS 337. Mm. 13–14, alto, notes 1–2 replaced by dotted whole-note in each m. in MS 121. M. 16, all parts, half-rest omitted in MS 121; bass, note 1 doubled at octave below in MS 337. M. 18, tenor, notes 2–3 replaced by dotted half-note in MS 121. M. 20, bass, note 1, flat is present in MS 337.

[42.] Canto di lanzi sonatori di rubechine

Source of music: MS Magl. XIX.141, fols. 96v–97.
Sources containing text only: Mk; Panc. 1; R2; IX.
Transcription of music according to MS 141. Text taken from MS 141.

Mm. 1–2, soprano part is unclear in MS 141. M. 25, alto, extra half-note (g') inserted after note 2 in MS 141.

[43.] Canto di lanzi venturieri

Author of text: Guglielmo detto il Giuggiola.
Sources of music: MS Magl. XIX.141, fols. 118v–119; MS Banco Rari 337 (bass only, untexted), fol. 55v.
Sources containing text only: Mk; Panc. 1; R2; IX.
Transcription of music according to MS 141. Text taken from MS 141.

M. 31, bass, note 1 has no flat in MS 337.

Acknowledgments

The editor would like to acknowledge the overall assistance and many valuable suggestions from the staff of the publisher. A special word of thanks goes also to Mr. Frank Carone for his help in preparing the synopses of texts.

July 1981

Joseph J. Gallucci, Jr.
Seattle, Washington

Notes

1. *Tutti i trionfi, carri, mascheeate [sic] ò canti carnascialeschi* (Florence: [Lorenzo Torrentino], 1559), p. iii.

2. For further biographical information see Frank A. D'Accone, "A Documentary History of Music at the Florentine Cathedral and Baptistry during the Fifteenth Century" (Ph.D. diss., Harvard University, 1960), I: 47–59.

3. Ibid., pp. 67–70.

4. Federico Ghisi, "Poesie musicali italiane: Canzonette a ballo, strambotti, frottole, canti e trionfi carnascialeschi," *Note d'archivio per la storia musicale* XVI (1939): 40–67.

5. A complete inventory with concordances can be found in the editor's "Festival Music in Florence, ca. 1480–ca. 1520: Canti carnascialeschi, Trionfi, and Related Forms" (Ph.D. diss., Harvard University, 1966), I: 103–122.

6. Ibid., I: 91–99.

7. Ibid., I: 236.

8. *Libro primo delle laudi spirituali da diversi eccell. e divoti autori, antiche e moderni composte . . .* , collected and edited by Serafino Razzi (Venice, 1563).

9. Two of these five concordances are with the same pieces in both manuscripts. See Gallucci, "Festival Music in Florence," I: 236–237.

10. Charles S. Singleton, ed., *Canti carnascialeschi del rinascimento*, Scrittori d'Italia, No. 159 (Bari, 1936), pp. 459-468.

11. See Gallucci, "Festival Music in Florence."

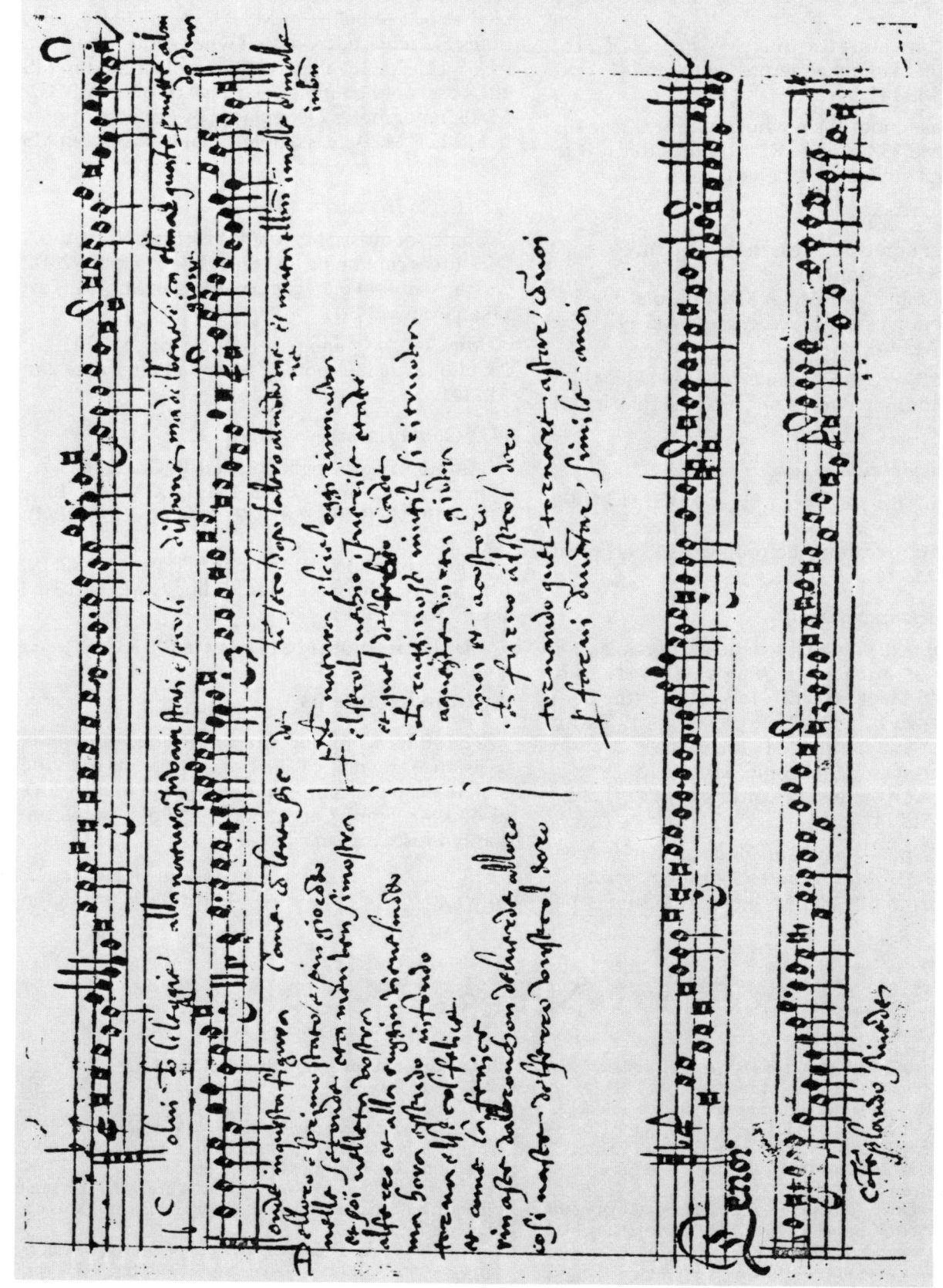

Plate I. *Trionfo della compagnia del Broncone* (soprano and tenor).
Florence: Biblioteca Nazionale Centrale, MS Magliabechiano XIX.141, fol. 88v.

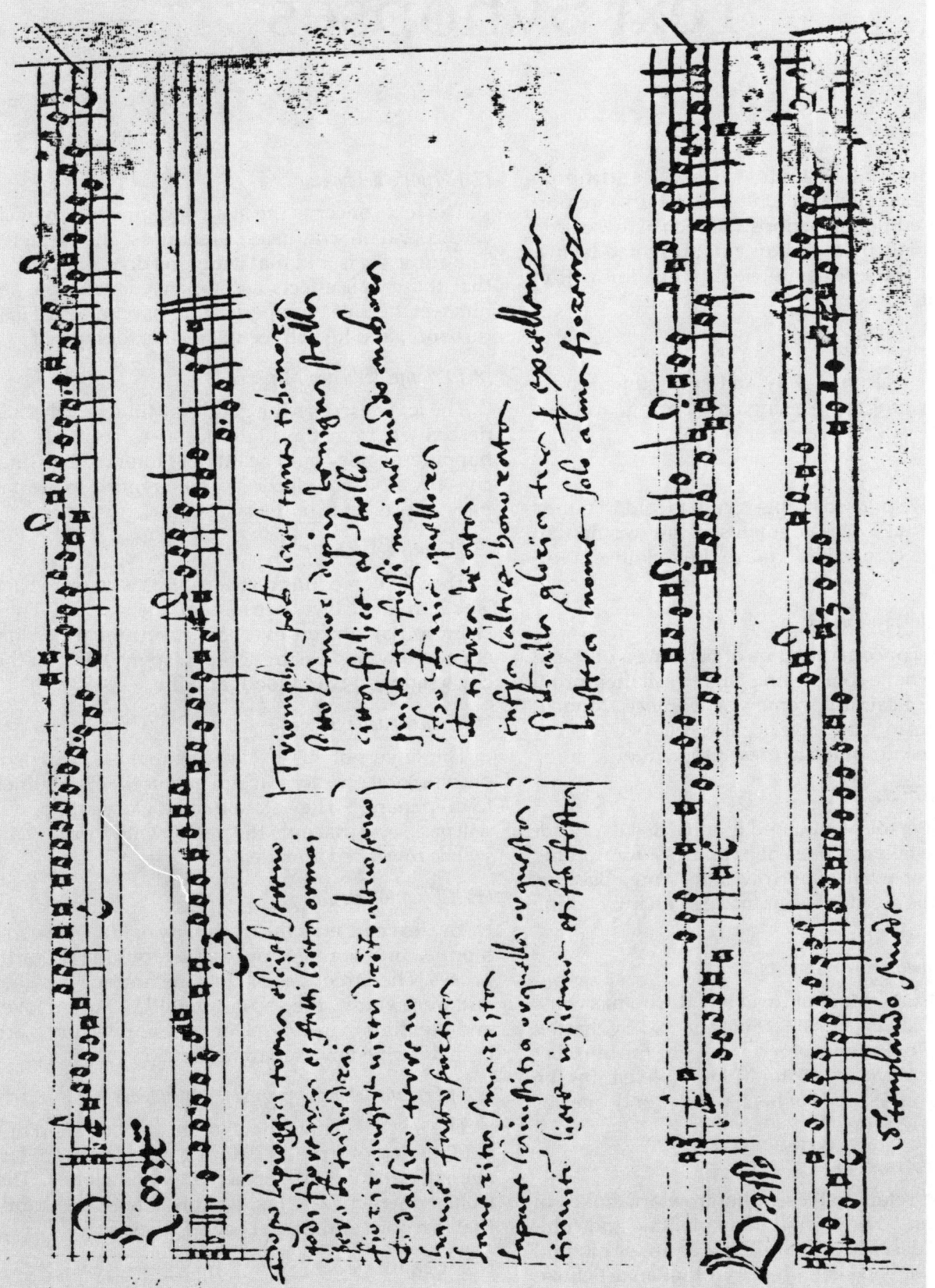

Plate II. *Trionfo della compagnia del Broncone* (alto and bass).
Florence: Biblioteca Nazionale Centrale, MS Magliabechiano XIX.141, fol. 89.

Text Synopses

Complete Italian texts, with all additional stanzas, are given with each piece in the score portion of this edition. A synopsis of each of these texts has been made by the editor and presented below. Authors of these texts are cited, when known, in the Critical Notes.

[1.] *"Ben venga maggio"*

The text welcomes May and springtime, and it speaks of young people singing, dancing, and reveling in this special season of love.

[2.] *Canto dei sarti*

Tailors are praised in this text. It is said that they will gladly take measurements of the women attending the carnival and make their clothes to order.

[3.] *Canto de' profumieri*

The text concerns vendors of perfumes, oils, and soaps who have come from Spain to sell their products to the beautiful women of Florence. Miraculous powers to soothe every pain and to solve every problem are attributed to these preparations.

[4.] *Trionfo di Bacco*

The text extols youth, and it urges that every advantage be taken of present happiness, for nothing is known of what tomorrow may bring. Bacchus and Ariadne are glorified as models of happy young lovers.

[5.] *Canto del mòro di Granata*

A handsome Moor of royal blood who has come from Granada is the subject of this text. Sympathy from the Florentine women is sought for him, because he is a victim of the Moorish defeat by the Spaniards in 1492, and of his 100 wives only one has remained with him.

[6.] *Canto de' cardoni*

The text refers to those who grow artichokes in their gardens. The techniques of planting and cultivation are described, as well as the proper method of eating the vegetable. It is said that an artichoke eaten without salt is as unexciting as a woman who goes to the carnival with her own husband.

[7.] *Trionfo del vaglio*

The text concerns the state of depression, which causes disdain, confusion, weariness, and torment. The audience is told that if anyone does not believe that these evil effects accompany depression, let him test the idea by experiencing psychological disturbance, and he will see the results for himself.

[8.] *Trionfo della dea Minerva*

The text describes the goddess Minerva, who has descended from the highest star to celebrate the happiness, glory, and beauty of Florence. The final civic triumph, the election of a Florentine to the papacy, is predicted in the last stanza.

[9.] *Canto de' diavoli*

The subjects of this text are spirits who were banished from heaven because of their pride. They claim to have taken over the government of Florence, and with pleasure accept responsibility for the city's sadness, war, blood, and fire.

[10.] *Carro della morte*

The singers of this text are costumed as dead people who ride on a wagon and exhort the Florentines to do penance. They state that all glory and pomp will pass, and that only the person with a pure heart will be rewarded after death.

[11.] *Trionfo dell'età*

The text concerns the mutability of life: the years, months, and hours go on, and everything on earth passes. The three ages of life—the first age of sweet and pure youth, the second period of ardent love, and the third mature time of fame and victory—are each described in a separate stanza.

[12.] *Trionfo della compagnia del Broncone*

The text proclaims that Florence, following a difficult period of strife, is entering now a new golden age greater than any of her previous glories. The *broncone* symbolizes this, for it is a large tree trunk that is reborn and sprouts new leaves.

[13.] *Canto delle dèe*

The goddesses Juno, Citherea, Minerva, and Venus are described. Each is claimed to have given special traits and gifts to Florence in order to make the city an earthly paradise.

[14.] *Trionfo d'amore e gelosia*

The text deals with the evils of jealousy, especially its ability to destroy real love. It says that both jealousy and love are present in each of us, and only by seeking love to the exclusion of jealousy can we attain true freedom and happiness.

[15.] *Canto di cacciatori*

The text refers to a group of hunters who practice their activity for the sheer pleasure of it. Neither mud nor rain can deter them from going to the fields with their dogs to pursue wild beasts.

[16.] *Canto di cacciatori che erano pastori e ninfe*

The subjects of this text are hunters who come upon beautiful nymphs and handsome shepherds in the fields. The sweet music that the nymphs and shepherds produce so captivates the hunters that they attribute musical qualities to all of nature.

[17.] *Canto dei capi tondi*

The text describes "round heads," a pejorative term for impudent, faithless men. The city of Florence is warned to rid itself of such types, because they are indeed "bad seed."

[18.] *Trionfo di diavoli*

The text describes fallen spirits who have fled from hell, the place of "eternal night," in order to warn the Florentine women of what happens to evil persons after death. The women are told that only while living can one act so as to merit eternal happiness.

[19.] *Canto de' disamorati*

The text refers to men disappointed in love, and it takes a highly uncomplimentary view of women. It says that only youth or money can hold a woman's affections, and man's fidelity, intellect, and gentleness are worth nothing. Woman is described as vain and inconstant by nature—proud, greedy, and ungrateful, pursuing the one who flees from her and scorning him who has always loved her.

[20.] *Canto di dominatori*

The text gives advice to those who would be rulers, stressing the uncertainties that accompany holding power over others. Rulers are urged to avoid listening to adulation; they should try instead to understand the truth and to hold always in their hands the bridle of reason.

[21.] *Canto di donne maestre di far cacio*

Women who are experts at making cheese are described. The process of manufacture is explained step-by-step, and the necessary attributes of those practicing this art are listed: great care, cleanliness, good eyesight, and patience.

[22.] *Canto di fanciulle in casa*

The text concerns young ladies who must remain in the house by their fathers' orders. They want to come out to meet their lovers, for their beauty is appreciated whether seen or not. They describe their desire to return love as beautiful, right, and natural.

[23.] *Canto della fortuna*

The text states that fortune governs all our lives and the entire world; not even a leaf falls without its will. Fortune is the hope of all who despair as well as the happiness of those who are content.

[24.] *Canto dei giudei*

The text refers to Jews, who are allowed to spend only three days in Florence. They taught the Florentines the art of cloth-making, and now the Florentines have taken away all their business. They hope at least to collect on past debts.

[25.] *Canto delle ninfe*

The text is addressed to an illustrious and gracious lord (presumably the ruler of Florence), who has received all of his character traits as special gifts from the various gods and goddesses of mythology.

[26.] *Canto delle parete*

The art of catching birds is the subject of this text. The women at the carnival are instructed on the proper method of using a decoy so that the birds will come into the net.

[27.] *Canto di pastori bacchiatori di bassette*

The text concerns shepherds who have decided to live according to nature. Dissatisfied with the fact that everything in life passes and not even wisdom or ingenuity is lasting, they seek a new country and kingdom wherein they will pursue a different lifestyle.

[28.] *Canto di pescatori a lenza*

The text describes those who have found true contentment by becoming fishermen. They know all the techniques for catching fish, but state that the big ones are most easily caught with a fishing line.

[29.] Canto della pomata

The text concerns the miraculous powers of an ointment which the singers have brought from their own country to the women in Florence. It comes from the fat of young animals and is especially beneficial to ease the pain of swollen muscles.

[30.] Canto dei poveri che accattano per carità

The text describes the poor who beg for charity. The implication is that poverty is the result of disappointment in love, and the women of Florence are urged to love always with fidelity so that they may receive a reward from heaven.

[31.] Canto della prudenza

The text is addressed to Prudence, the "exalted and agreeable lady," with the entreaty that she show favor to those who seek her assistance. She is said to reward each person who follows the straight and true pathway in this life.

[32.] Trionfo della prudenza

In this text Prudence and all who follow her laws are exalted. Prudence is said to govern all the world and to contend for allegiance with the two great enemies of life, expectation and fear.

[33.] Trionfo dei quattro tempi dell'anno

The text describes the four seasons of the year and concerns the inevitable passage of time. The Florentine women are urged to recognize and appreciate the treasure of youth, for it will all too soon be taken away by old age.

[34.] Canto dei romiti

The subjects of this text are hermits who were happy in their solitude but decided to leave the country in order to experience more normal social relationships. They had been away from human society for so long that they became unbalanced, believing that human society was much better than their previous life.

[35.] Canto de' savi

The text refers to those who have acquired true wisdom, saying that they are not subject to the vicissitudes of fortune or chance and do not need gold or silver; their wisdom suffices to give them contentment.

[36.] Trionfo delle tre parche

The text describes three parks in which childhood, youth, and old age are resplendent. Childhood gives life to the heart, youth sustains that life, and old age is the inevitable end to our prejudices or good deeds.

[37.] Canto di uccellatori alle starne

The text concerns those who hunt partridges. It is said to be most important that their hounds have long noses and comely heads, because these are perfect indicators of skill in tracking down the birds.

[38.] Canto di uomini vecchi allegri e goditori

The text refers to elderly men who are undaunted by their age and are still eager to have a good time at the carnival. They do not apologize if some think them to be crazy, for both the insane and the wise must soon face the end of life.

[39.] Canto di zingane

The text concerns gypsies who have come to Florence to beg for alms. They are in a wretched state, worn out by the ravages of rain and snow, and they have arrived with children in their arms. They will sing and dance in exchange for charity.

[40.] "Guardate al cielo, el ciel creò costei"

The subject of this text is a mythological goddess, the "goddess of the other gods," from whom everything in the world receives life. This text also expresses the mutability theme as it describes the brevity of life and the concept of one generation following another.

[41.] Canto di lanzi pellegrini

The text refers to a group of *lanzi*, German mercenary troops, who have come to Florence from Rome, where they made a pilgrimage. They received so many indulgences in Rome that all of their sins have been forgiven. They ask for charity, since they are poor and unfortunate strangers in Florence.

[42.] Canto di lanzi sonatori di rubechine

The text concerns German troops who play the rebec, a bowed string instrument with pear-shaped body. They are said to produce a sweetness of sound that is divine, and they love to play, dance, and sing.

[43.] Canto di lanzi venturieri

The text refers to German troops who are true adventurers. They are always ready to go to war, and their custom is to travel all over carrying their weapons with them.

FLORENTINE FESTIVAL MUSIC
1480–1520

[1.] "Ben venga maggio"

Venite alla frescura
delli verdi arbuscelli.
Ogni bella è sicura
fra tanti damigelli;
che le fiere e gli uccelli
ardon d'amore il maggio.

Chi è giovane e bella
deh non sie punto acerba,
che non si rinnovella
l'età, come fa l'erba:
nessuna stia superba
all'amadore il maggio.

Ciascuna balli e canti
di questa schiera nostra.
Ecco che i dolci amanti
van per voi, belle, in giostra:
qual dura a lor si mostra
farà sfiorire il maggio.

Per prender le donzelle
si son gli amanti armati.
Arrendetevi, belle,
a'vostri innamorati;
rendete e' cuor furati,
non fate guerra il maggio.

Chi l'altrui core invola
ad altrui doni el core.
Ma chi è quel che vola?
È l'angiolel d'amore,
che viene a far onore
con voi, donzelle, al maggio.

Amor ne vien ridendo
con rose e gigli in testa,
e vien di voi caendo.
Fattegli, o belle, festa
qual sarà la più presta
a dargli e' fior del maggio?

Ben venga il peregrino.
Amor, che ne comandi?
Che al suo amante il crino
ogni bella ingrillandi;
che le zitelle e grandi
s'innamoran di maggio.

[2.] Canto dei sarti

Per tagliar in punto et bene,
la misura in mano pigliamo;
tucti panni per le schine,
dopie sol panno mictiamo:
poi coll'occhi nui guardamo
se gli è dentro taglio honesto.

Quando el panno non è assucto,
non se pò mai ben tagliare;
fase taglio tristo et bructo
se non se lassa rasuctare:
quando è assucto se pò fare
tucti li tagli, et fansi presto.

Poi pregamo dui o tre volte,
le mani sopra quel panno;
perchè el pelo spesso volta
inganna como multi sanno:
nostro s'avvia pur el danno
se guastassemo qualche veste.

Per donzelle et per garzoni
nui tagliamo omne rubecta;
mastri siam da far juppuni:
chi à vasi, in mani cel mecta,
et se pur ne avessen frecta,
servirili bene et presto.

Basta solo aver veduto
quanta robba vi po intrare;
non è mai un si sorignato,
che lo non facciamo victo stare:
ma bisogna operare
un'altra arte inverso questi.

[3.] Canto de' profumieri

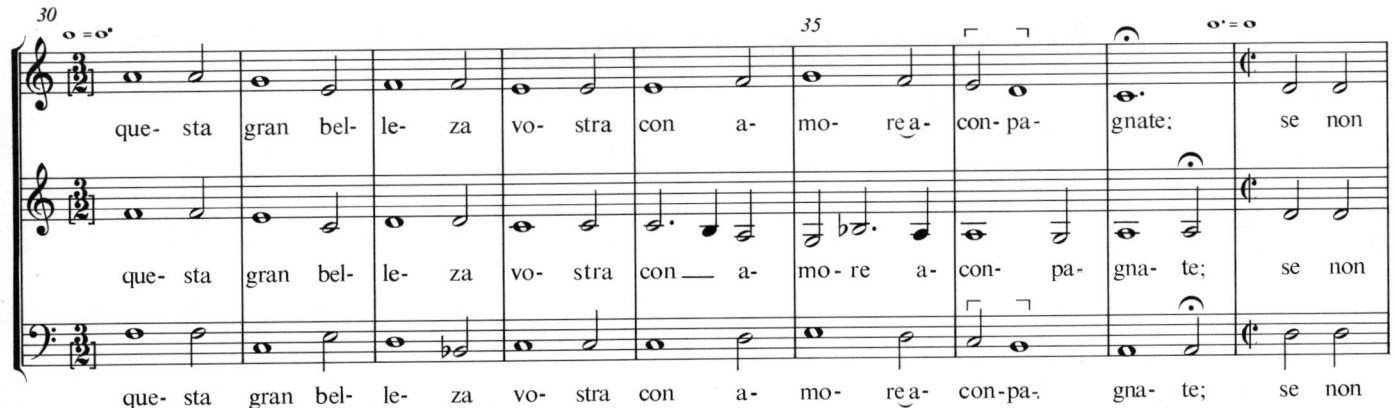

Secondo e nostri costumi
userèno anchor de nudoi;
uselletti oli et profummi,
donne belle, abbiàn con noi:
ànno odor suave, et poi
molto aiuton la natura,
se c'è donna alcuna dura
contra a amor, la farà senza.

Quanto è una buona spanna
uselletti begli abbiàno,
se dicessi: altri c'inghanna,
noi ve gli porrèno in mano;
ritti alluogho gli mettiàno,
nella punta acceso è el focho:
onde spargi e appocho appocho
dolze odor che à gran potenza.

Or dell'olio vogliàn dire,
à odore et virtù tanta,
che fa altri risentire
dal capo fino alla pianta;
l'olio è una cosa santa,
se stillato è in buona boccia:
escie fuora a goccia a goccia;
se più pena, à più potenza.

L'olio sana ogni dolore
et risolve ogni dureza,
tira asse tutto l'umore
tra del menbro la caldeza;
penetrando da dolceza
quanto più forte stropicci:
se ài triemiti o capricci,
usa l'olio et sarai senza.

Noi abbiàno un buon sapone
che fa saponata assai,
fregha un pezo ove e si pone:
se più meni, più n'arai;
ev'egli achaduto mai,
donne, aver l'anella strette?
Col sapon si cava et mette
quoce un pocho: patientia!

Donne, c'o che abbiàno è vostro;
se d'amore voi siate accese,
metterèn l'olio di nostro,
ugnerèno a nostre spese;
abbiàno olio del paese,
gelsi, aranci, et munguì:
se vi piace, proviàn qui:
fate questa sperienza.

[4.] Trionfo di Bacco

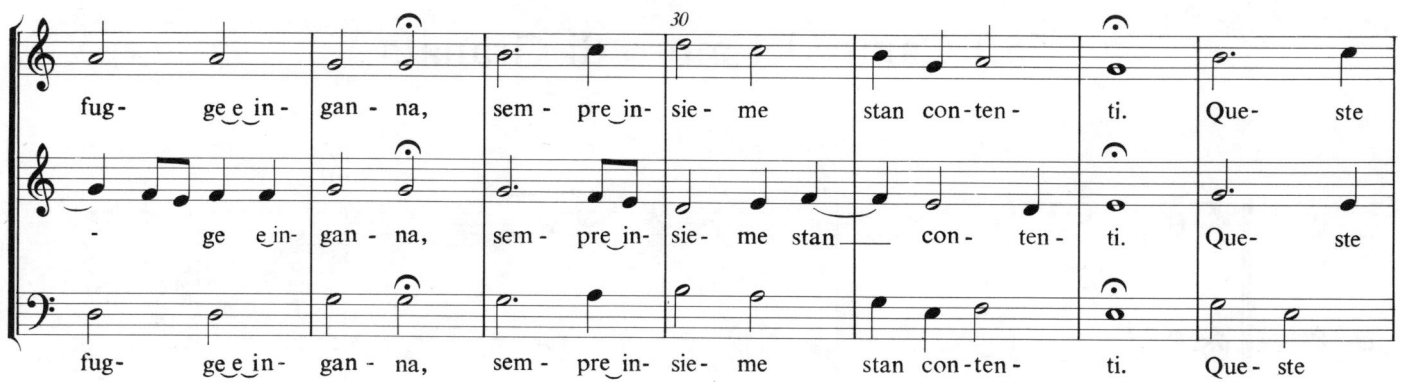

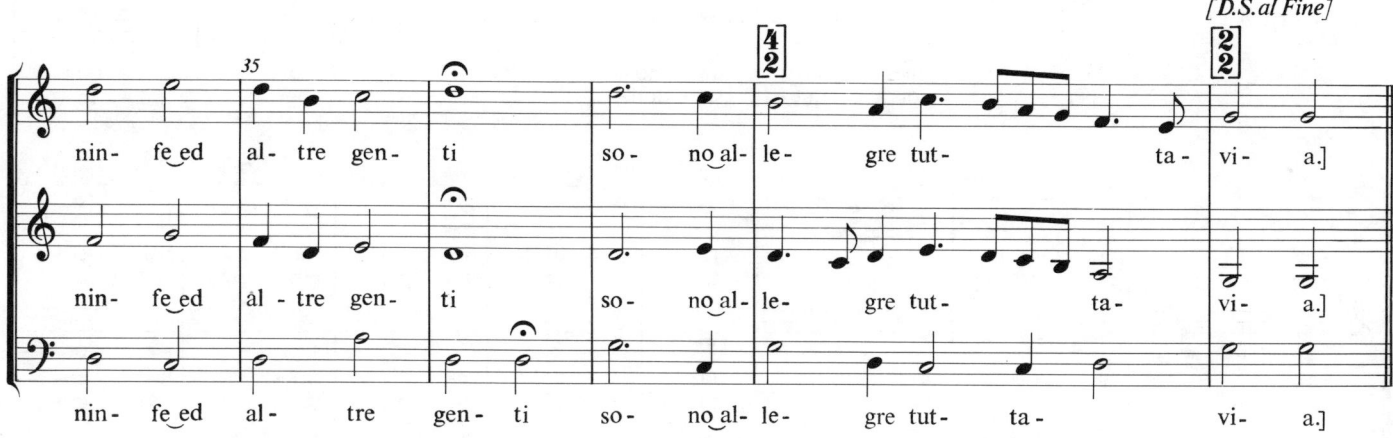

Questi lieti satiretti,
delle ninfe innamorati,
per caverne e per boschetti
han lor posto cento agguati;
or da Bacco riscaldati,
ballon, salton tuttavia.
Chi vuol esser lieto, sia:
di doman non c'è certezza.

Queste ninfe anche hanno caro
da lor esser ingannate:
non può fare a Amor riparo,
se non gente rozze e ingrate:
ora insieme mescolate
suonon, canton tuttavia.
Chi vuol esser lieto, sia:
di doman non c'è certezza.

Questa soma, che vien drieto
sopra l'asino, è Sileno:
cosi vecchio è ebbro e lieto,
gia di carne e d'anni pieno;
se non può star ritto, almeno
ride e gode tuttavia.
Chi vuol esser lieto, sia:
di doman non c'è certezza.

Mida vien drieto a costoro:
cio che tocca, oro diventa.
E che giova aver tesoro,
s'altri poi non si contenta?
Che dolcezza vuoi che senta
chi ha sete tuttavia?
Chi vuol esser lieto, sia:
di doman non c'è certezza.

Ciascun apra ben gli orecchi,
di doman nessun si paschi;
oggi siàn, giovani e vecchi,
lieti ognun, femmine e maschi;
ogni tristo pensier caschi:
facciam festa tuttavia.
Chi vuol esser lieto, sia:
di doman non c'è certezza.

Donne e giovinetti amanti,
viva Bacco e viva Amore!
Ciascun suoni, balli e canti!
Arda di dolcezza il core!
Non fatica, non dolore!
Cio c'ha a esser, convien sia.
Chi vuol esser lieto, sia:
di doman non c'è certezza.

[5.] Canto del mòro di Granata

Cent' moglie àve el misero infelice!
Donne belle, pietà di lui vi prenda;
a ciascuna di voi del suo dar lice:
quanto lo fate, ch'altri non lo intenda,
guardatevi da chi 'l fa et poi el dice;
nessun c'è ch'oggi merito buon renda,
et chi da voi riceve più vantaggio,
più ne parla, et mancho è prudente et saggio.

Non sa el mòro parlare in fiorentino,
ma intende presto chi l'accenna o tocha:
inparerà poi el misero meschino,
quand'una gli darà la lingua in bocha.
Benchè crede altra fede el peregrino,
non vi guardate, e' sare' cosa sciocha:
come bagniato fia nelle vostr'aque,
rinegherà la fè che già gli piaque.

Qual di voi, donne, fie la più amante,
che di sè facci gratia, un dono a quella
questo mòro farà del suo turbante
di tela, che giamai fu la più bella,
et grosso et sodo et fanne volte tante
che stracha questa moglie vechierella:
per compier fornimenti, questo è desso;
a voi et vostre figlie sarà messo.

Ampolle abbiàno d'una certa aqua piene:
gittate nelle vostre carne giova;
mostrar come si fa saria pur bene,
l'è l'arte sua et non gli è cosa nuova:
quando l'aqua del mòro fuor ne viene
dolcemente par proprio dal ciel piova;
aqua lanfa è, con muscho, chiara et netta:
sprite ove volete vi si metta.

Molt'altre cose, o belle donne, ancora,
che 'l mòro porta sotto, vi presenta;
ma del vostro benigne siate allora:
con una moglie e' povero huomo stenta!
Fate una carità, inanzi mòra
vostra belleza, quale hor ora è spenta.
Orsù, pigliate delle cose nostre,
che 'l mòro a doppio vuol poi delle vostre.

[6.] Canto de' cardoni

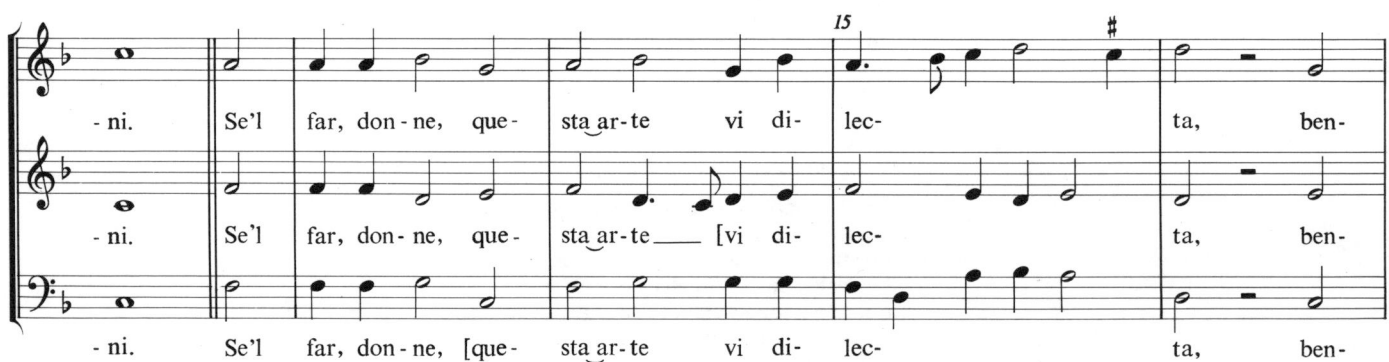
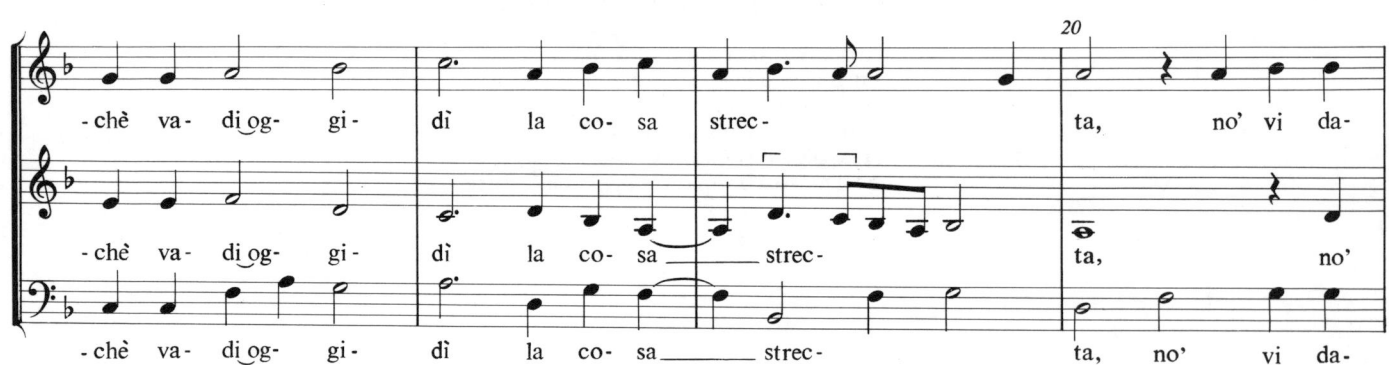

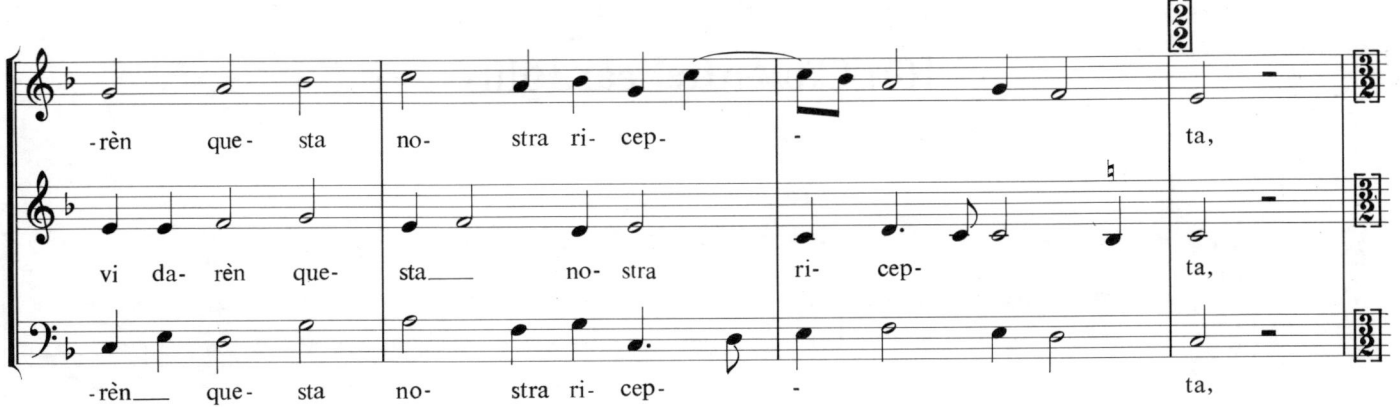

Il modo a culturar un cotal fructo
è gittar forte il seme per l'asciutto,
chè quando e' piove, o il seme va mal tutto,
o produce scrignuti et stran cardoni.

Bisogna prima d'intorno sarchiarlo,
pigliar le foglie in man et poi legarlo,
coprirlo et ritto ritto sotterrarlo:
ècci qualcun che lo pianta bocconi.

Vuol esser il cardon di tal misura,
un palmo o poco più, che la nattura
smaltiri non può sì gran cosa et sì dura,
benchè a noi piaccion sempre e gran bocconi.

Quando si coglie, grosso a compimento
fate che sia, perchè ne' picciol drento
sugo non è, et si mangiono a stento,
et sono sciochi assai più che' melloni.

Ècci qualche golosa che cel toglie
di mano, c'è non che il gambo, insin le foglie
si mangia, tanto è ingorda alle suo voglie;
benchè ghiotti ne sono anche e garconi.

Tanto è mangiar il cardon senza sale
quanto far col marito il carnovale,
chè 'l sugo per se stesso tanto vale
quanto alle non gen(te?) gli stasoni.

Usonsi innanzi passo, o vuo' di drieto,
benchè talor dinanzi habb[in divieto];
ma innanzi et dopo gl'usa l'huom discreto,
secondo tempo et sempremai son buoni.

[7.] Trionfo del vaglio

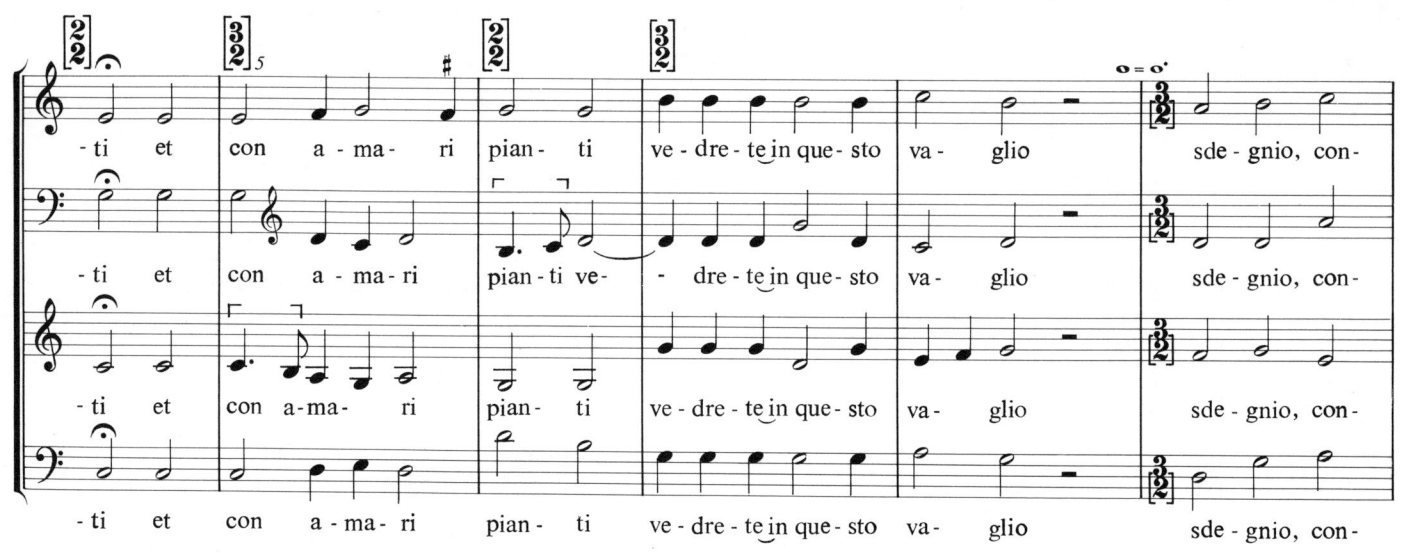

Non ci mandate seghala nè vena:
qui entron biade grosse
che reghono alle scosse
et son di miglior mena;
et anche a mala pena
si truova chi rimangha drento al vaglio.

Chi entra in questo vaglio et chi se n'esce,
chi piange et chi sospira,
e 'l vaglio sempre gira
et la forza ci cresce:
chi del suo mal gl'incresce,
fugha la furia e 'l pericol del vaglio.

Se mille volte el dì el vaglio enpiàno,
mille volte si vòta:
perchè el vaglio si squota,
si vede a mano a mano
coperto tutto el piano
di gente che escon de' buchi del vaglio.

Chi non si sente bene granito et forte,
non facci di sè pruova;
e 'l pentir poi non giova
o cerchar miglior sorte:
me' sarebbe la morte
che sopportare e tormenti del vaglio.

[8.] Trionfo della dea Minerva

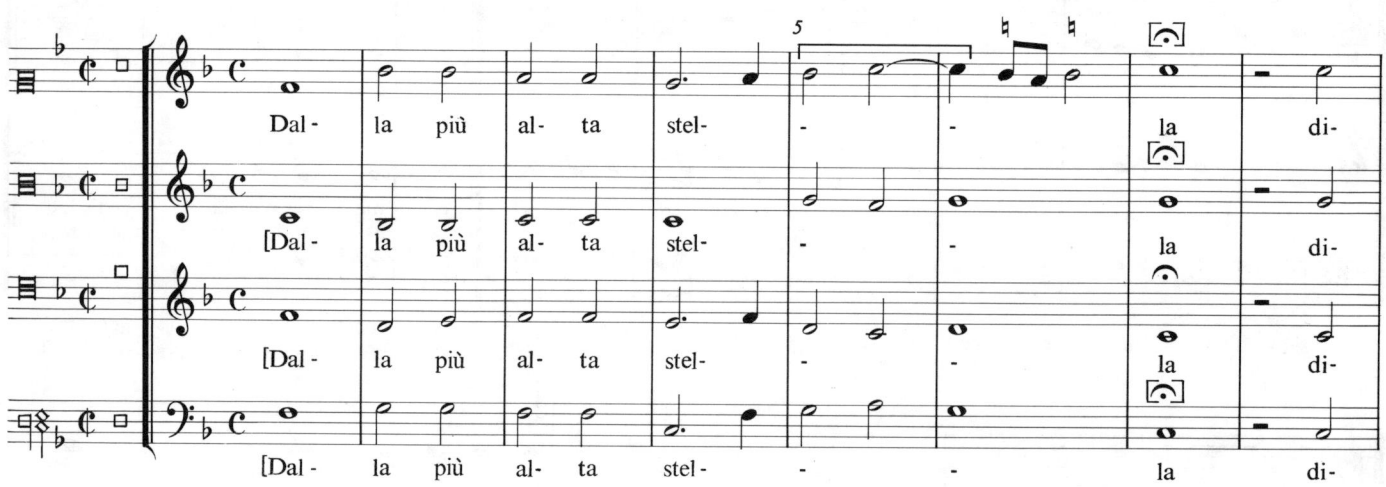

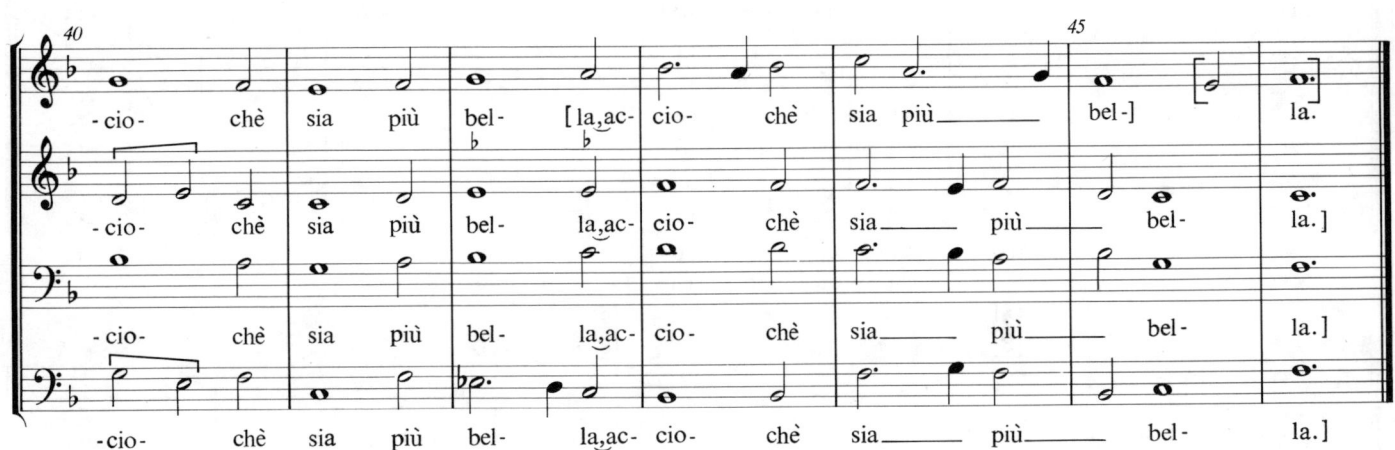

Pocha ventura giova
a chi mancha el favor di queste donne,
e tu, Fiorenza, el sai,
che queste son le tuo ferme colonne;
la gratia che tu ài,
d'altronde non la trai
che dall'ingegnio, di che ognior fai pruova.

Le stelle sono stiave
del senno, et lui governa le fortune;
or ài, Fiorenza, quello
che disiavi tanto e'n tante lune:
l'onorato chappello.
Verrà tenpo novello,
ch'arai le tre corone et le duo chiave.

[9.] Canto de' diavoli

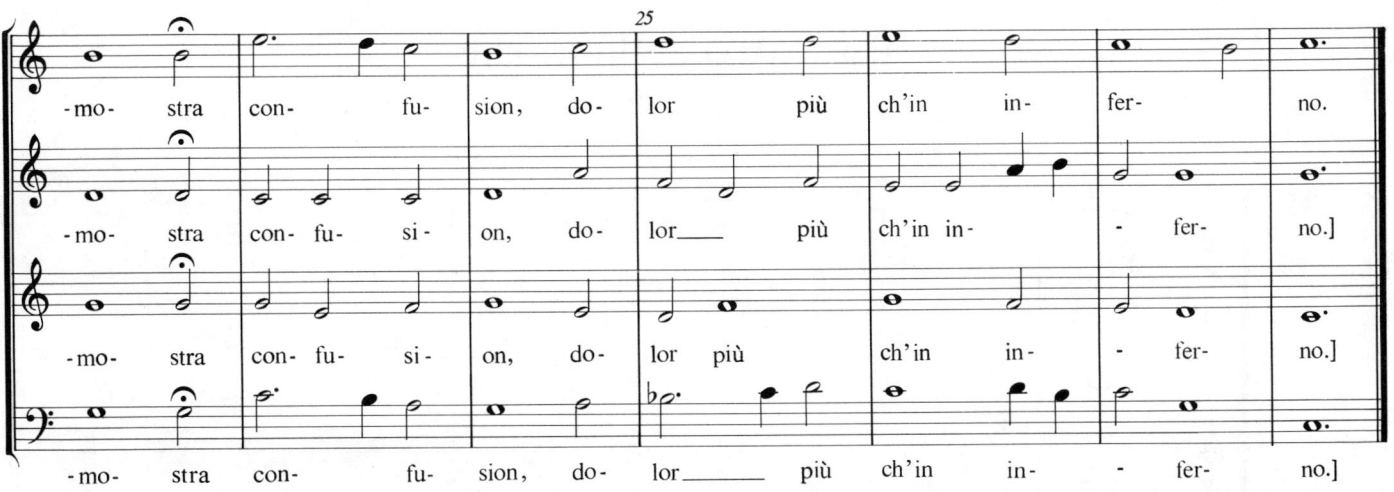

Et fama et guerra et sangue et fiamma et focho,
sopra ciascun mortale
abbiàn messo nel mondo appocho appocho;
et questo carnovale
vegniàno a far con voi,
perchè di ciascun male
fumo et siàno et sarèn principio noi.

Plutone è questo et Proserpina è quella,
ch'allato se gli posa,
donna sopr'ogni donna d'amor bella,
amor vince ogni cosa;
però vinse costui
che mai non si riposa,
perch'altri facci quel ha fatto lui.

Ogni contento et scontento d'amore
da noi è generato,
el pianto e 'l riso e 'l diletto e 'l dolore;
chi fussi inamorato
segua el nostro volere,
et sarà contentato
perchè d'ogni mal far pigliàn piacere.

[10.] Carro della morte

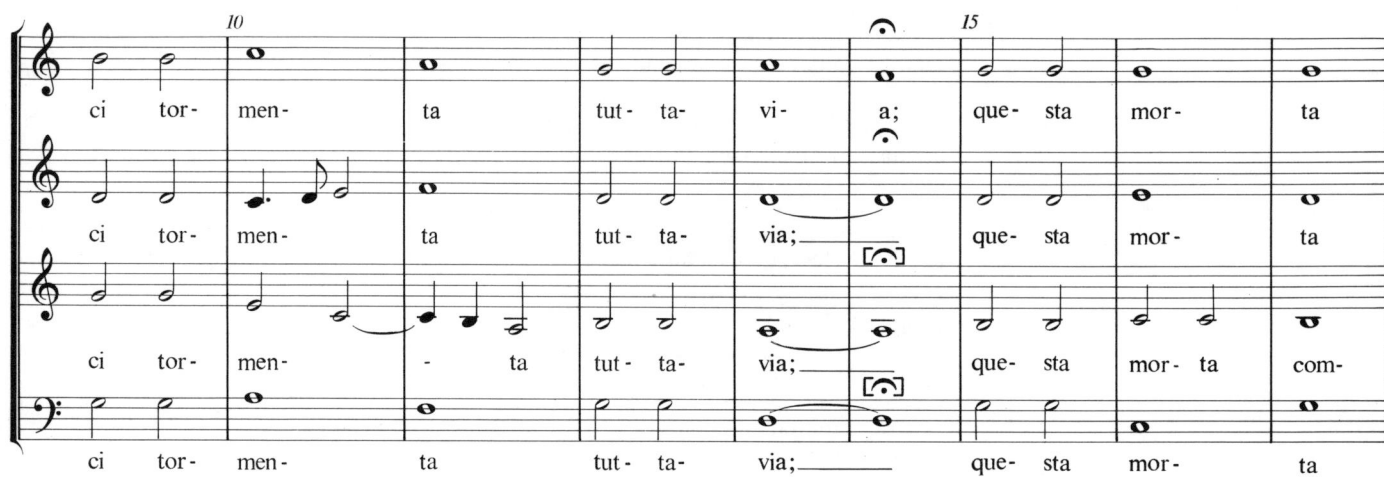

Ancor noi per carnovale
nostri amor giuàn cantando;
e così di male in male
andavàn moltiplicando:
hor pel mondo andiam gridando
"penitenza, penitenza."

Ciechi, stolti & insensati,
ogni cosa il tempo fura:
pompe, gloria, honori e stati
passan tutti e nulla dura;
e nel fin la sepoltura
ci fa far la penitenza.

Questa falce che portiamo,
l'universo al fin contrista,
ma di vita in vita andiamo:
sia la vita o buona o trista,
ogni ben del cielo acquista
chi di qua fa penitenza.

Gran tormento e gran dolore
ha di là colui ch'è ingrato,
ma chi la pietoso il core
è fra noi molto honorato;
vuolsi amar quando altr'è amato,
per non far poi penitenza.

Se vivendo ciascun muore,
se morendo ogn'alma ha vita,
il Signore d'ogni signore
questa legge ha stabilita:
tutti havete a far partita;
pazienza, pazienza!

[11.] Trionfo dell'età

L'altro grado è el terzo segnio:
pien di fama et di vettoria,
questa età guida ogni regnio;
cercha al mondo honore et gloria;
fa perfetta la memoria,
l'huom prudente et bene acorto,
purchè guidi el legnio in porto,
come fa chi vuole honore.

Vien l'età d'amore ardendo,
c'ogni cor gentile invita:
gioventù, lieta, ridendo,
vien cantando et molto ardita.
O che dolze et bella vita!
Chi [va] a chaccia et chi fa versi,
chi d'amor non può tenersi,
tanto è fagho el suo bel fiore.

Risguardate, donne belle,
voi che siate in questo coro,
vedovette et damigelle:
non fu mai più bel tesoro;
hoimè, che forza d'oro
non raquista quel che è perso!
Quando el tempo è fatto adverso,
l'huom conoscie el ciecho errore.

Così el tenpo speza et rompe
questa nostra vita breve;
tante glorie et tante ponpe
strugge el tenpo più che neve;
vien la morte oscura et greve,
con suo falce miete et taglia:
non è guanto, piastra o maglia
che non ronpa el suo furore.

Voi che siate in questa vita,
non perdete el tempo invano:
ogni gloria è poi finita,
quando morti et spenti siàno;
torna el monte spesso in piaano;
et però chi 'l tempo perde
nell'età govuine et verde
pocho dura et presto mòre.

[12.] Trionfo della compagnia del Broncone

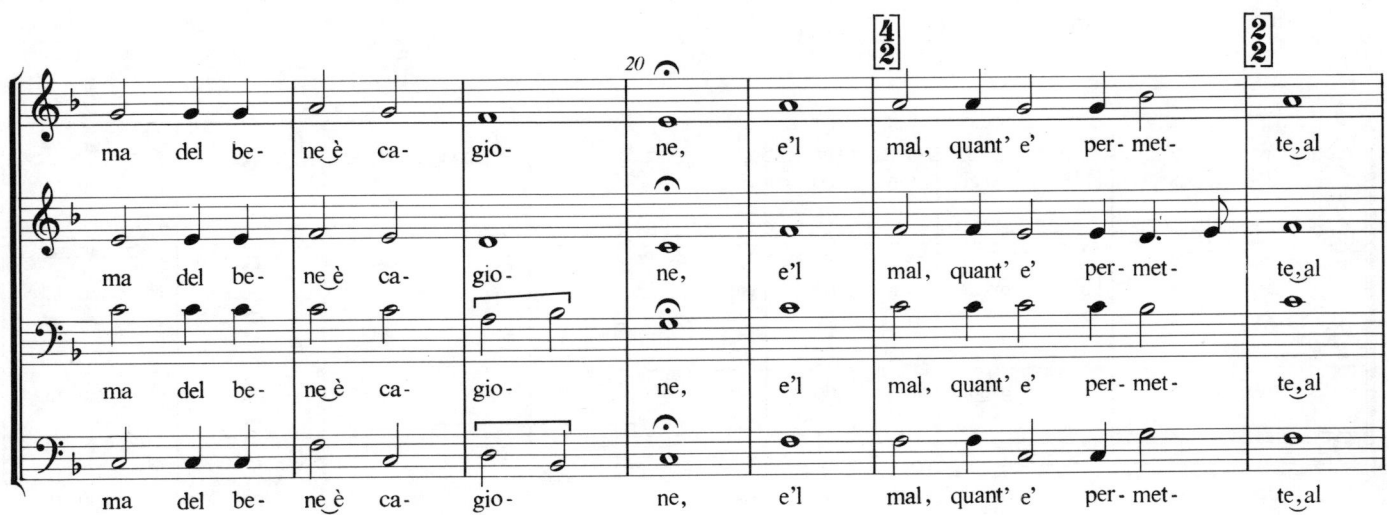

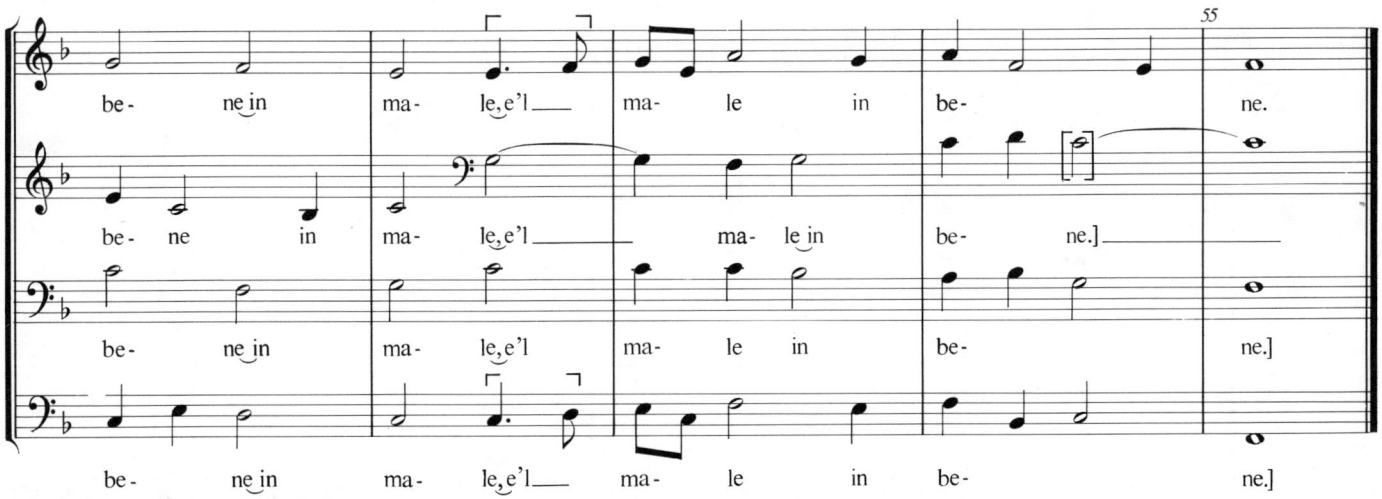

Dell'oro el primo stato è più giocondo,
nelle seconde età men ben si mostra;
et poi nell'età vostra
al ferro et alla ruggin viene 'l mondo:
ma hora, essendo in fondo,
torna el secol felice;
et come la fenice,
rinasce dal bronchon del verde alloro:
così nasce del ferro un secol d'oro.

Perchè natura el ciel oggi rinnuova
e 'l secol vechio in puerile etade,
et quel del ferro cade,
che rugginoso, inutil si ritruova,
a queste virtù giova,
a noi et a costoro
che furno al secol d'oro,
tornando quel, tornare a star con voi
per farvi diventar simile a noi.

Dopo la pioggia torna el ciel sereno:
godi, Fiorenza, et fàtti lieta ormai,
però che tu vedrai
fiorir queste virtù drento al tuo seno,
che dal sito terreno
havien fatto partita:
la verità smarrita,
la pace, la iustitia, or quella or questa,
t'inviton liete insieme e ti fan festa.

Triompha, pochè 'l ciel tanto ti honora
sotto 'l favor di più benigna stella.
Città felice et bella,
più che tu fussi mai nel mondo anchora:
echo che vien quell'ora
che ti farà beata
e 'n fra l'altre onorata,
sì, che alla gloria tua per excellenza
basterà 'l nome solo, alma Fiorenza.

[13.] Canto delle dèe

[Heinrich] Isa[a]c

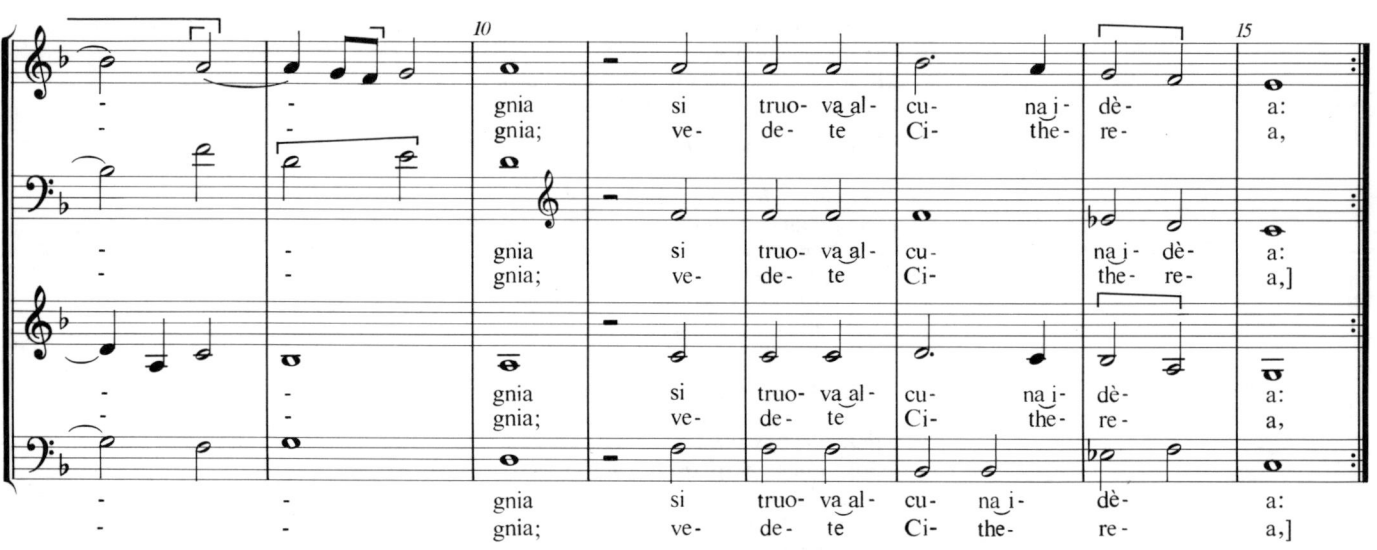
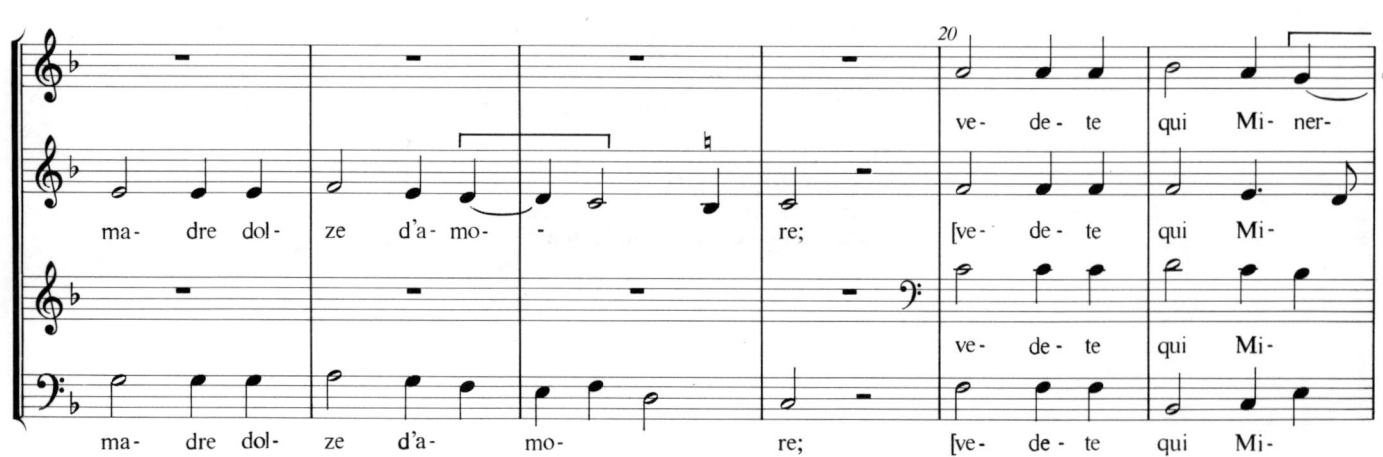

Fiorenza, tu sarai la più famosa
cipta che vegha el sole;
di lor presenza sarai gloriosa:
Iunon tuo stato vuole
crescere et in concordia
tener donne et mariti;
e ciptadini uniti
terrà sanza discordia;
farà el popol fruir fuor d'ogni usanza,
sano et gagliardo et sempre in abbondanza.

Minerva saggia ci darà vittoria
contro a nimici in guerra;
faratti trionphar con somma gloria,
et per mare et per terra,
in tutte le buone arte
o di mano o d'ingegno:
sola passera el segnio,
felice in ogni parte,
tochando el cielo colla superba chioma,
Fiorenza bella, figluola di Roma.

Ma Vener bella sempre in canti e 'n feste,
in balli e 'n noze et mostre,
in varie foggie et nuove sopraveste,
in torniamenti et giostre
[farà 'l popol fiorito;]
farà galante et bebbe
tutte donne et donzelle,
con amorosa vista;
terrà sempre Fiorenza in canti et riso
et dirassi: Fiorenza è 'l paradiso!

[14.] Trionfo d'amore e gelosia

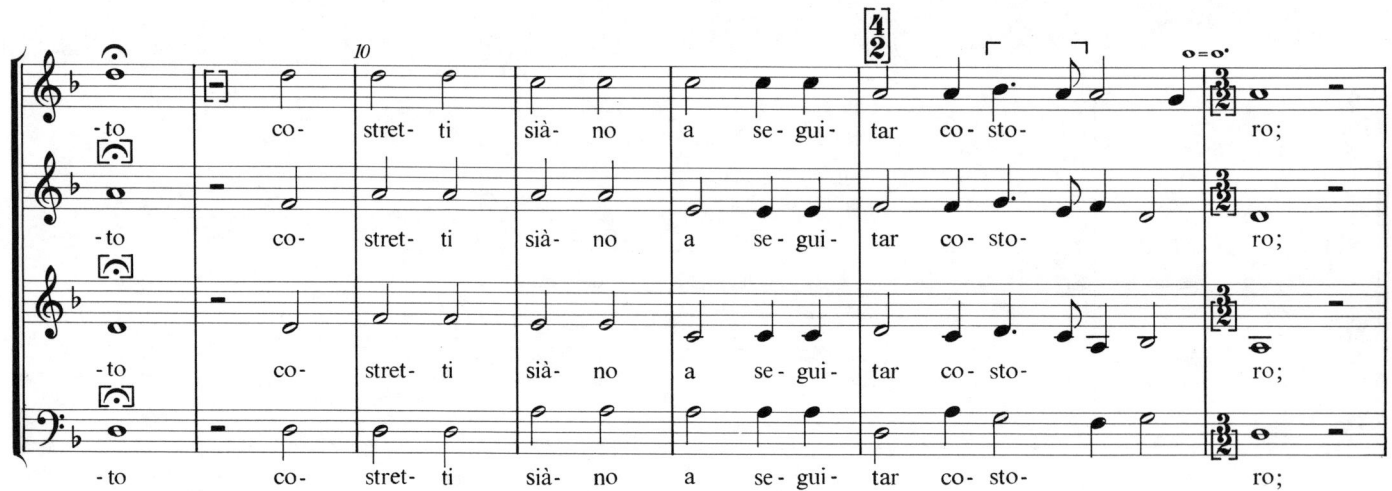

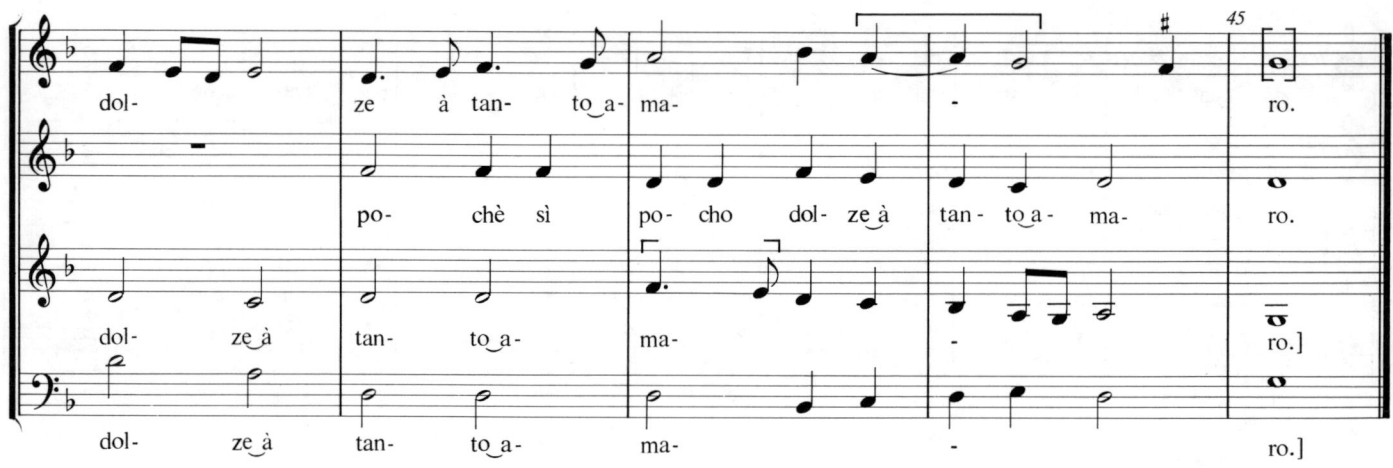

Naquon costoro insieme antichamente
et così insieme vivono et morranno;
quasi sopr'ogni gente,
come vedete, iuriditione hanno;
benchè ogniun lietamente
servirebbe ad amore, che è signior nostro,
se non fussi quell'altro orrendo mostro.

Per la forma et per l'abito s'intende
chi coste' sia et gl'effetti suo' fèri;
dal vestir ben conprende
ciascun gl'incerti et vari suo' pensieri;
testimonanza rende
la suo magreza e 'l suo colore anchora
com'altri sempre distrugge et divora.

Quatro vòlti à, perchè per tutto vuole
l'orechio suo, la bocha et gl'ochi porgere;
per l'amorose scole
ciò che si dice et fa, cercha di scorgere;
mai somno albergar suole,
ma sempre piange et sempremai mal v[ede],
et peggio pensa et a verun non crede.

Per me' vedere, gl'ochiali agl'ochi porta,
co' quali vien radoppiando el suo dolore,
perchè gli sono scorta,
veggiendo male, a mostrargliel maggiore;
di nulla si conforta,
ma 'l suo sospetto in infinito acrescie,
et dove un tratto albergha, mai non escie.

Con quella spada che la porta in mano
ferisce altrui, nè sana mai tal piagha,
et noi qui lo proviàno;
così sempre costei di mal s'appagha,
come detto v'abbiàno:
et però ciaschedun che liber sia,
fugha questa perversa gelosia.

[15.] Canto di cacciatori

Noi abbiàn certi brachetti
che son buoni sol da levare.
Benchè sieno molto perfetti,
gli sogliàno pocho operare.
Ma usiàn sol di bussare
dove sono lepre inmachiate,
et diàn lor certe frugate,
che le sbucon presto fuori.

Come e' n'è una scoperta,
e can nostri sgunzagliàno,
ch'alla china come all'erta,
gugner presto la veggiàno.
Di riscontro mai lasciàno
perchè el cane spesso l'erra;
la si spiana et stiaccia in terra
et può farsi cento errori.

Noi abbiàno alcuna volta
de' can nostri andar lasciati,
che la fiera alor s'è volta
et di sangue gli à machiati.
Et però son sì sdegniati
ch'alle golpe più non vanno:
benchè tal vitio non hanno
tutti e cani de' cacciatori.

Tutta l'arte del cacciare
nella perticha veggiàno.
Et però si vuol guardare
che el legniame non sia vano;
et tastalla ben con mano,
se ella à dura et soda vetta:
chè la pertica perfetta
fa valenti cacciatori.

[16.] Canto di cacciatori che erano pastori e ninfe

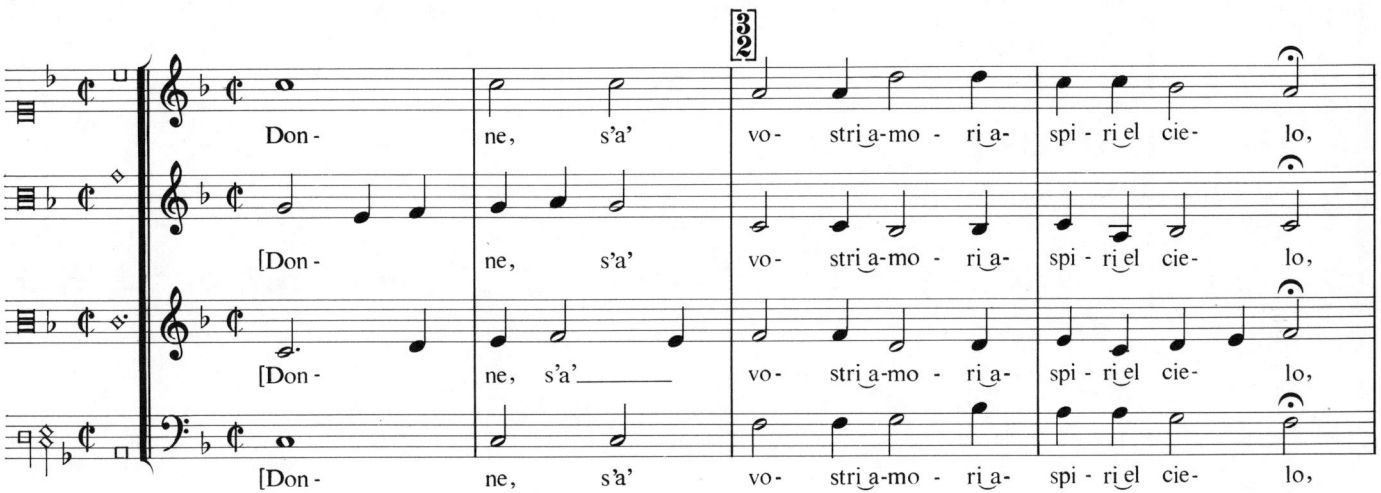

Quanto et qual lor concento sia,
per noi sprimer non puossi;
ma e fiumi al suon di lor dolze armonia
han fermi e' savi mossi:
noi perch'udirle apieno ciaschuna possi,
l'abbiàn dell'aspre selve tratte fòri.

Vedete questo lieto satiretto,
di dolze amor leghato,
che sol di consecrar lor sacro aspetto
è contento et beato;
e l'à sempre seguite in ciaschun lato,
nè star sanz'esse par che si rinquori.

El cielo, el paradiso et gli elementi
et tutti gl'animali
di musicha son pieni et di concenti,
e' corpi de' mortali:
rare cose è nel mondo nelle quali
non sien misura, musicha o tenori.

Ma perchè volar l'ore ognior si vede,
donne leggiadre et care,
tempo è costoro hormai vi faccin fede
di loro opre alte et rare:
dolze armonie sentirete, et pleclare,
da queste ninphe et suavi pastori.

[17.] Canto dei capi tondi

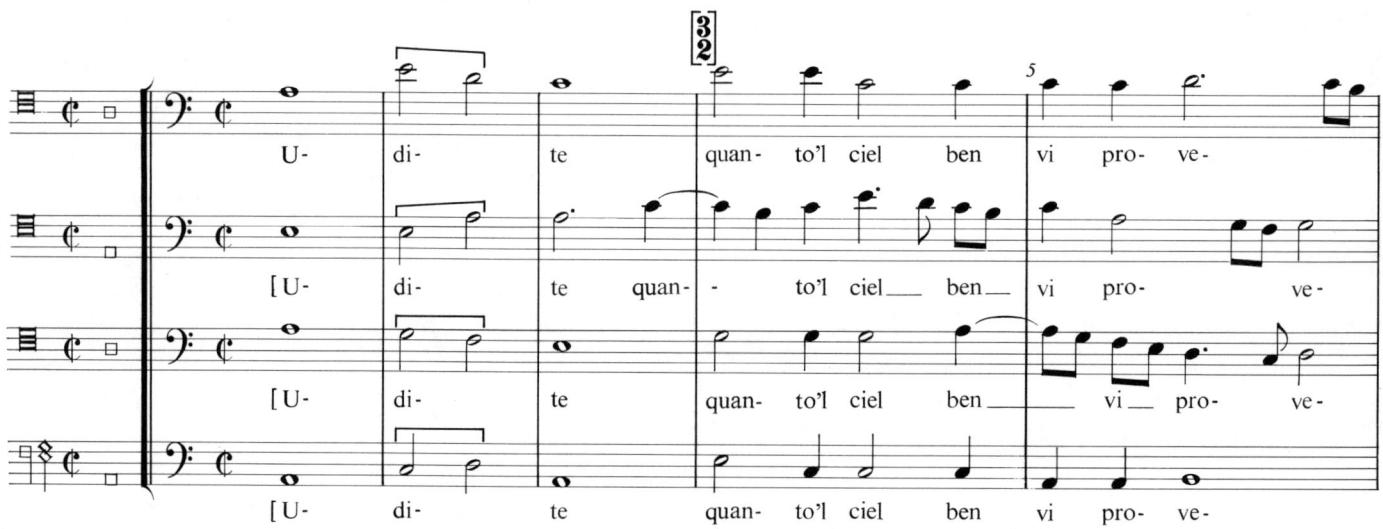

Voglion, per parer savi, conversare
con ciascun dotto, nobil, richo et degnio,
et lodar come quello et biasimare,
per mostrar più amor, più fede e 'ngegnio;
nè han piacere o sdegno
di beffe, strati parole aspre o buone,
ma faccendo el buffone
ciascuno achatta, toglie, usurpa et chiede.

Spesso l'opre d'altrui s'atribuischono;
et a chi me' lor fa, più ingrati sono;
et quel che è l'util loro quel favoriscono,
odiando chi gli scuopre et ciascun buono;
et per ogni vil dono
fan del no sì et del sì no con noi
et scusandosi poi
che 'l mondo degli inpronti esser si vede.

D'ogniuno et d'ogni cosa dicon male
et non confesson mai nessuno errore;
e primi a mensa, et uno per quatro vale;
gl'ultimi alla faticha et sanza amore;
et coll'altrui favore
voglion valersi et promettono assai,
ma non observon mai,
s'un più inpronto di lor non gli richiede.

Ben ti puo' gloriar, Fiorenza bella,
se 'n te non è di questa mal semenza:
ond'or che t'è propitia ogni altra stella,
se ne venissi alcun, dàgli licenzia;
che 'l dar loro audienza
ci tolse già tesori, onore et stato;
ma or più raquistato,
diàn del lor vitio in terra a ciascun fede.

[18.] Trionfo di diavoli

M. Alexander Coppinus
[Alessandro Coppini]

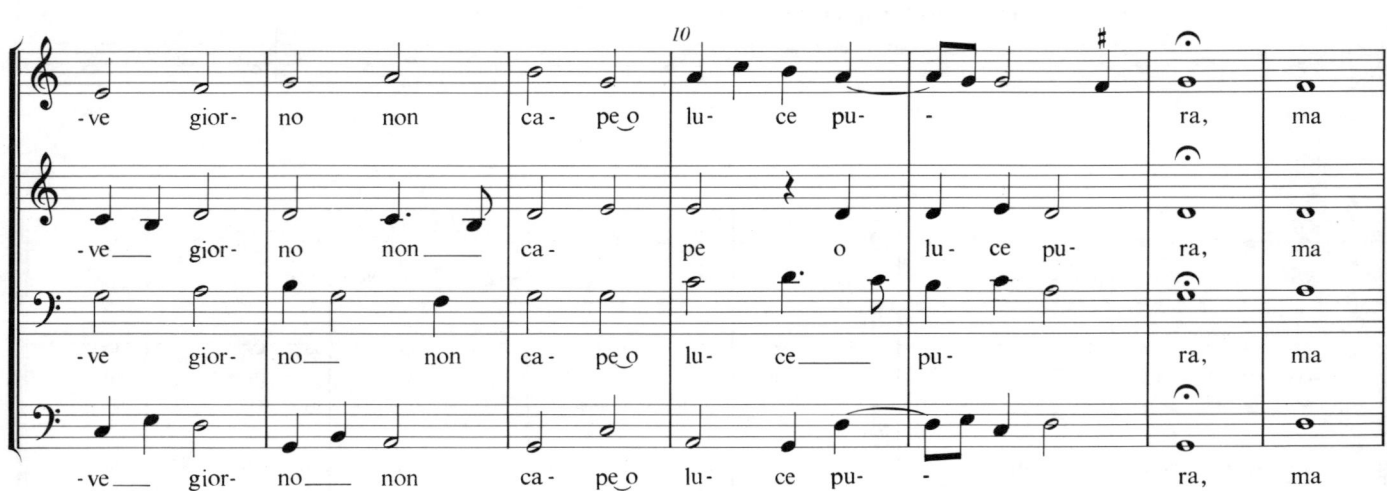
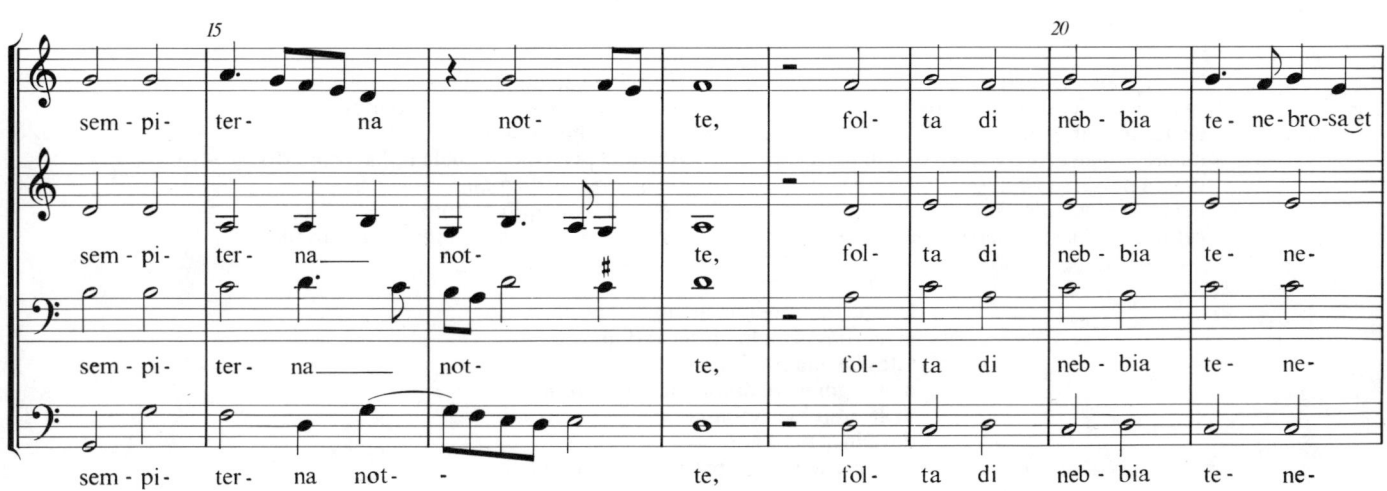

Noi eravàn di quegli
spirti beati del superno coro,
già tanto lieti et begli
quant'or siàn brutti et pien d'ogni martoro:
nostra perversa voglia
del cielo el ver tesoro
ci tolse et tien sommersi in pena e 'n doglia.

Non lievi alchun la vista
contro al principe suo, chè cotal merto
cotal premio s'aquista
da quel principe al quale nulla è coperto;
le nostre acerbe pene
vi sieno exemplo certo:
temer e amare chi 'l sommo sceptro tiene.

Donne, mentre che in vita
di meritar el cielo gratia vi dona,
fate che alla partita
non vegniate al dolor che sì ci sprona
dalla eternale ambascia,
dove insieme s'aduna
qualunque troppo prende o troppo lascia.

[19.] Canto de' disamorati

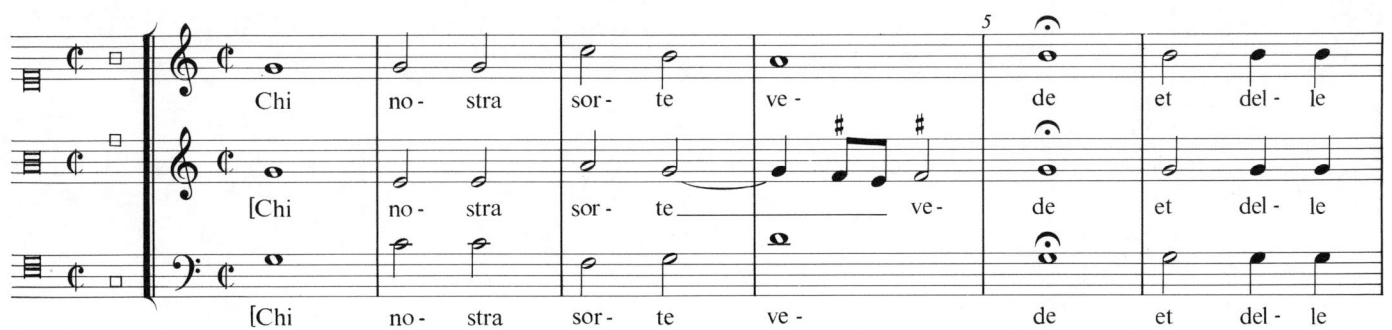
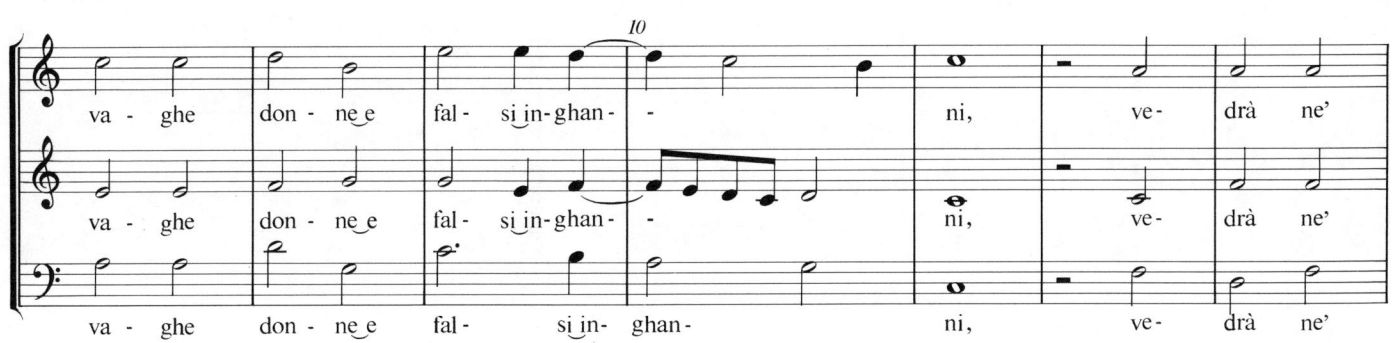
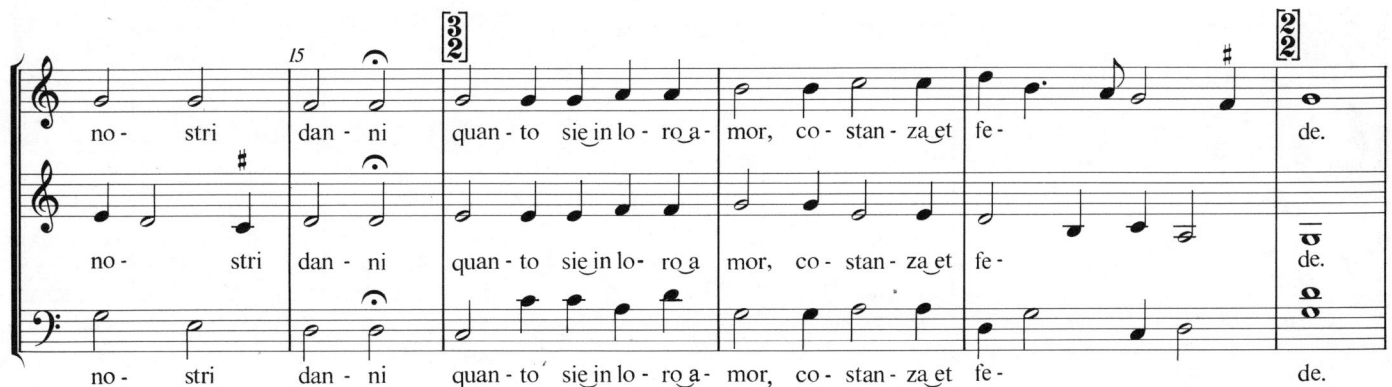

La donna è vana et mobil per natura,
superba, avara e 'ngrata;
pocho la vita d'altri o 'l suo honor cura,
quando è punto infiammata;
segue chi fugge, et chi l'à sempre amata
a in odio et lo rifiuta,
et con fortuna muta
nuovo amatore e 'l vechio lascia a piede.

Vaglion gli amanti loro come le biade,
con buchi larghi et stretti;
chi vola via, chi resta in gratia, et cade,
secondo lor diletti;
proverranno ora un pocho e giovinetti,
ch'ad in principio et fine
le lasseràn meschine,
recerchando ogni di più fresche prede.

Se non siàn così giovani et gagliardi,
el troppo sempre nuoce;
facciàno al tempo presto, adagio et tardi
tal che el bochon non quoce,
nè non vegniàno del popolazo in voce:
presto vedrèn vendette
di queste maladette,
et in altri troverrèn gratia et merzede.

[20.] Canto di dominatori

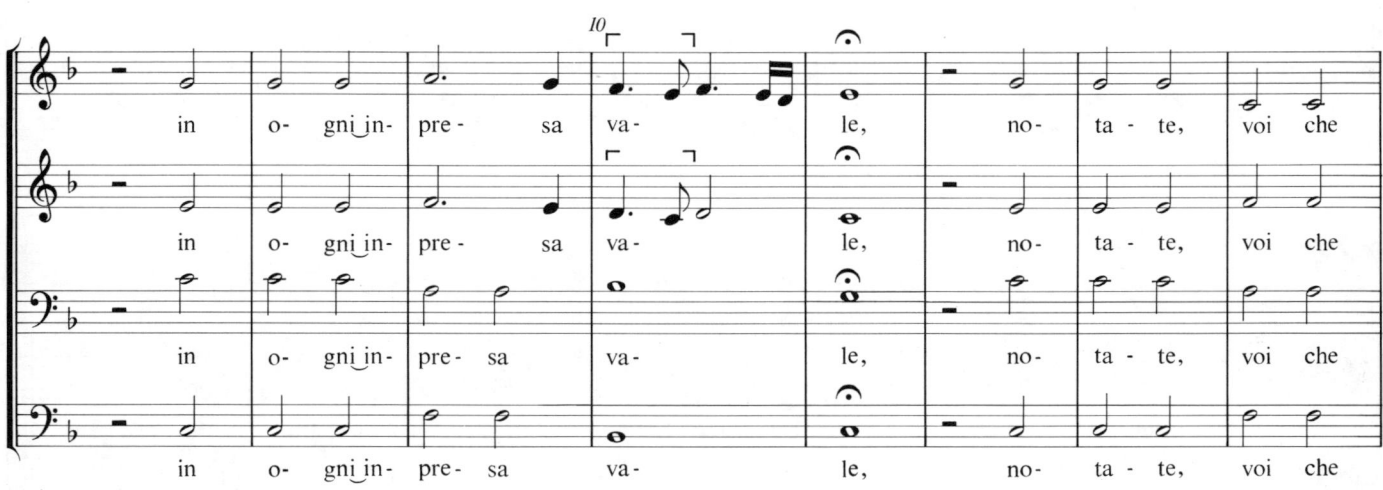

Ciascuno aspira all'alta signoria
come affelicità dello intelletto;
et la voglia desia
di bene in meglio ognira esser perfetto:
ma escie della via
perchè ciecha in confuso il suo ben vede:
così spesso inghannata al falso accede.

Se quel che vive in mediocle stato
conoscessi el pericol del regniare,
non più desiderato
sare' da quel, per non si contentare:
un picciol vento, un fiato
è il viver nostro, ov'ogni nodo scioglie
Fortuna, ch'a suo posta dà et toglie.

Però chi regnia questo exemplo prenda
et fuggha udir le molte adulatione;
et se può, el ver conprenda.
Dando in suo man la briglia alla ragione
chè, quanda la vicenda
gli mancha et viene el colpo di fortuna,
conturbato non sia da parte alcuna.

Segue dunque virtù chi vuol fuggire
el mal che questo nume agl'uman porgie:
con questa alto salire
si può, dove fortuna non lo scorgie:
ma quel che vuol dormire
nella ignoranza, a caso è sopragiunto
dallei et perde ogni cosa in un punto.

[21.] Canto di donne maestre di far cacio

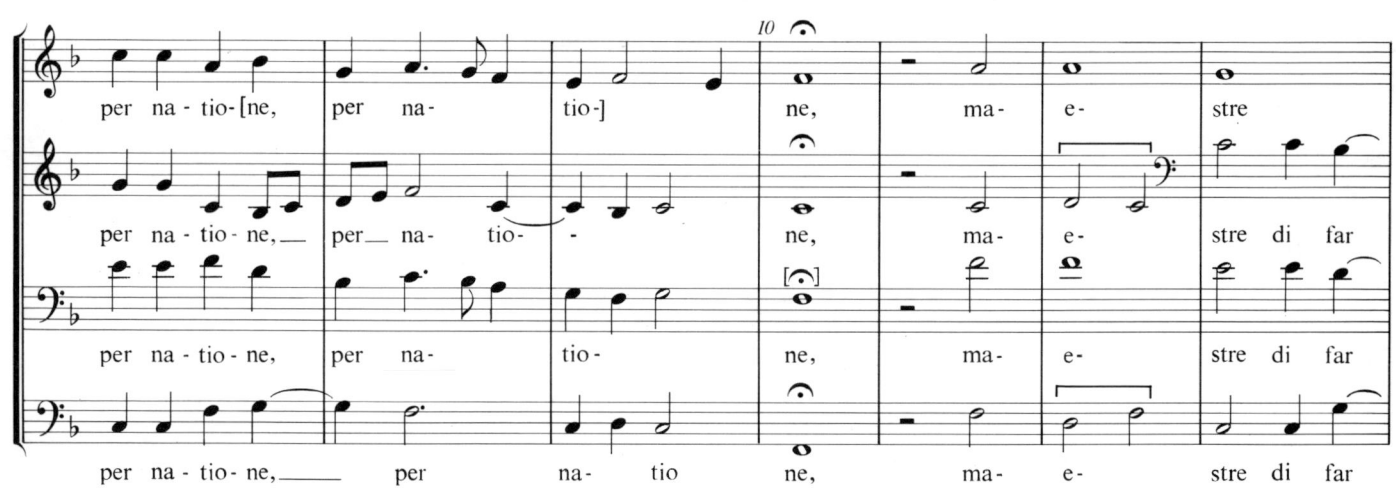
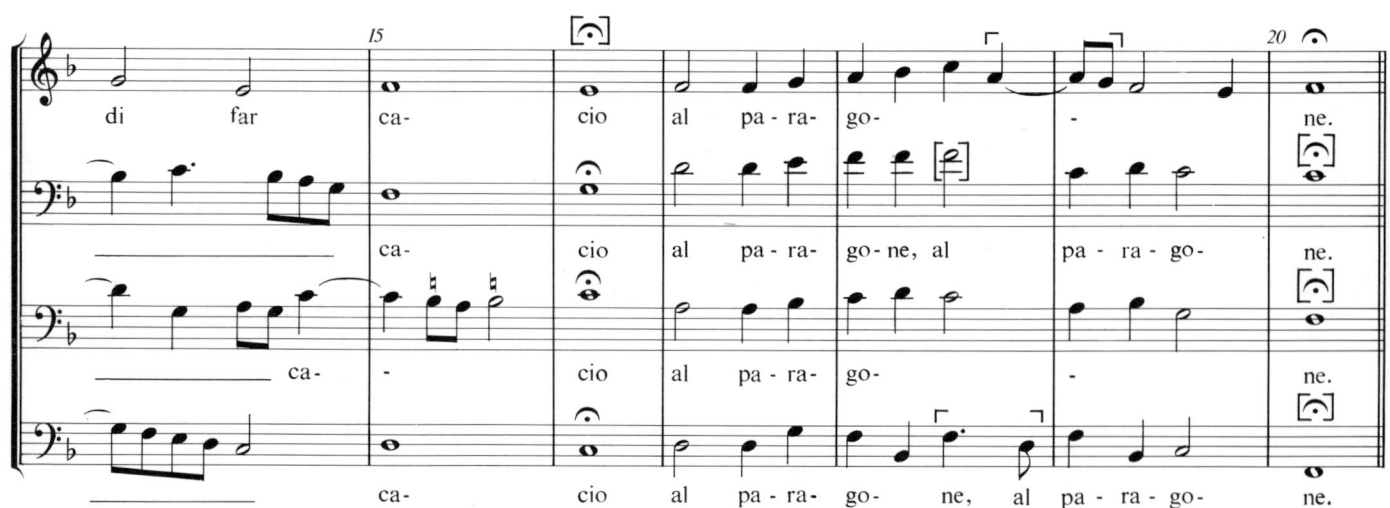

Bisognia prima aver tutto l'armento
rinchiuso fralle rete o 'n chasa drento,
pigliarne una per volta: o che contento
ha quella che è la prima a tal factione!

Presa che è l'una, qual sie qui di noi
gli apre le coscie et dalle poppe poi
prieme el latte nel vaso, tal che voi
ben quante noi il faresti in suo stagione.

O che piacere è quando torna el latte!
Et se in mezo del vaso entrar s'abbatte;
ma se la bestia alquanto si dibatte,
si perde el frutto a tal consolatione.

Sono alcune di quelle sì sdegniose
d'esser toche per tutto et paurose
che, quando le tochiàno, di strane cose
fanno, et ne piscia alcuna nel buglione.

Et se la pecorella è atenpata,
sta sopra 'l vaso che la par mura[ta],
tanto che la sie munta e sgoccol[ata]:
voi come noi sapete la cagione.

Come 'l vaso del latte è tutto pi[eno],
colasi et ponsi al fuoco, et vuole almen[o]
duo peze bianche, benche molte sieno
zanbrache che non han tal discretion[e].

Come 'l latte è rapreso nel vasello,
bisognia con duo mane trarlo di quello,
priemerlo, maneggiarlo et farlo bello,
formarlo et porlo asciutto nel gabbione.

La forma non vuole esser molto grande,
nè picho anche, perchè fuor si spande;
el troppo e 'l pocho guasta le vivande:
chi l'à a misura non à reprensione.

El nostro cacio in sè tutto è perfetto,
non troppo corto, lungo, largo o stretto,
grosso a ragion, ritondo, saldo et netto:
fra 'l terzo e 'l mezo piace a più persone.

Noi ne darèno attaglio e 'n tutti e modi
che voi volete, freschi, passi et sodi,
con prezo et sanza prezo, et ogniun godi:
et questi fien per mostra et per canpione.

[22.] Canto di fanciulle in casa

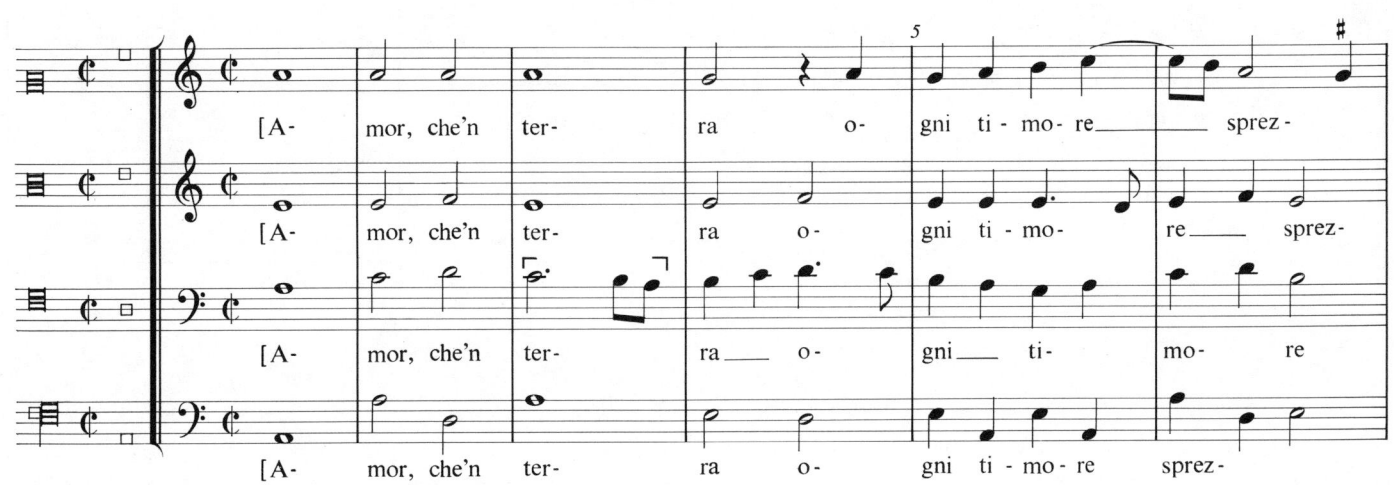
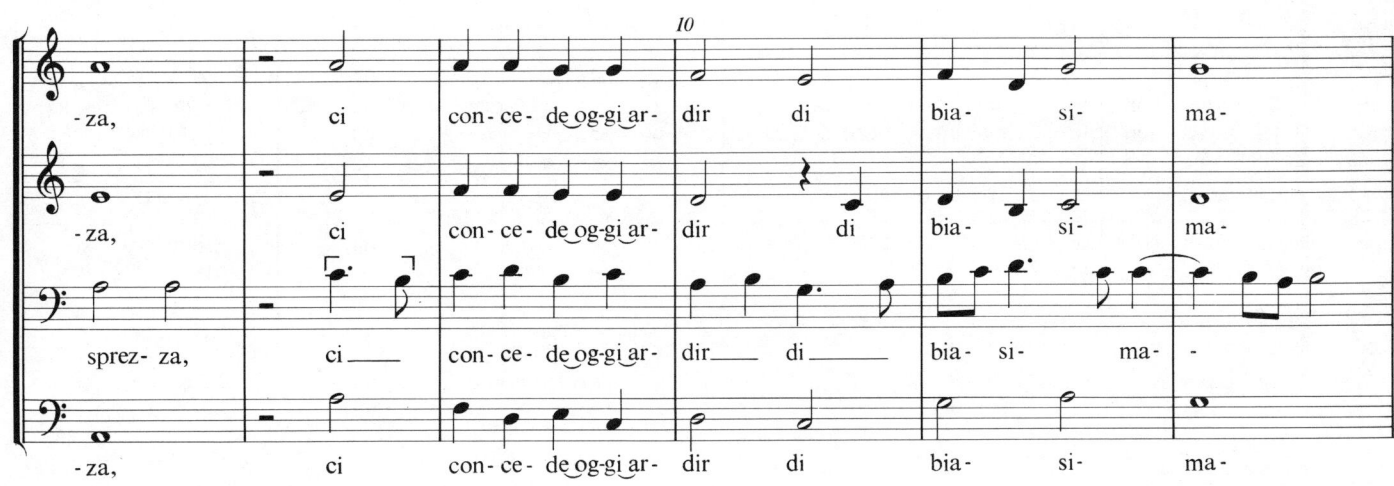

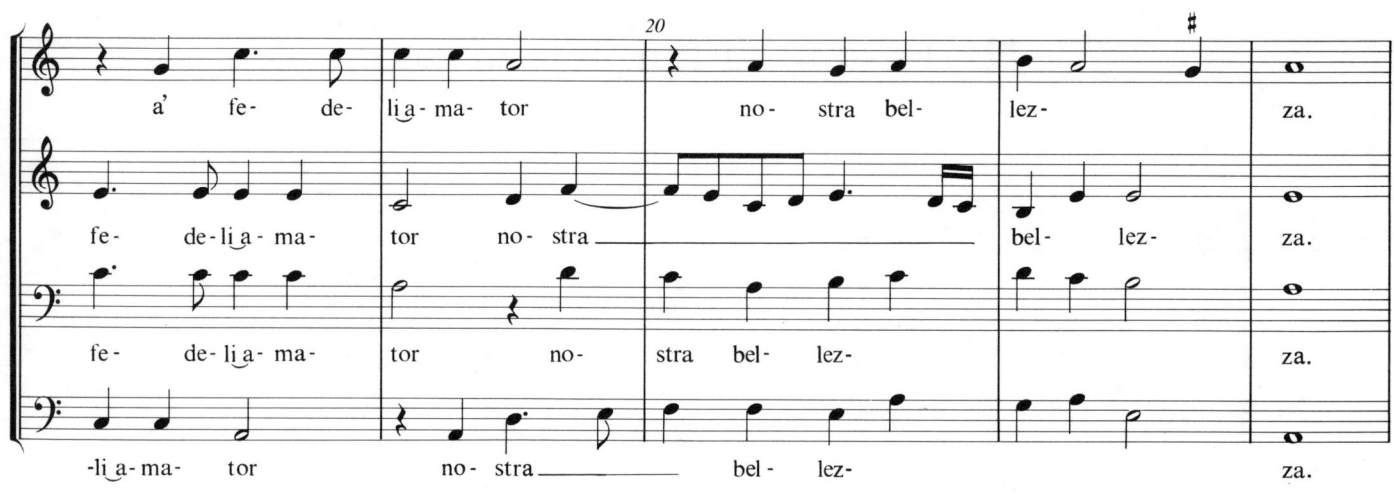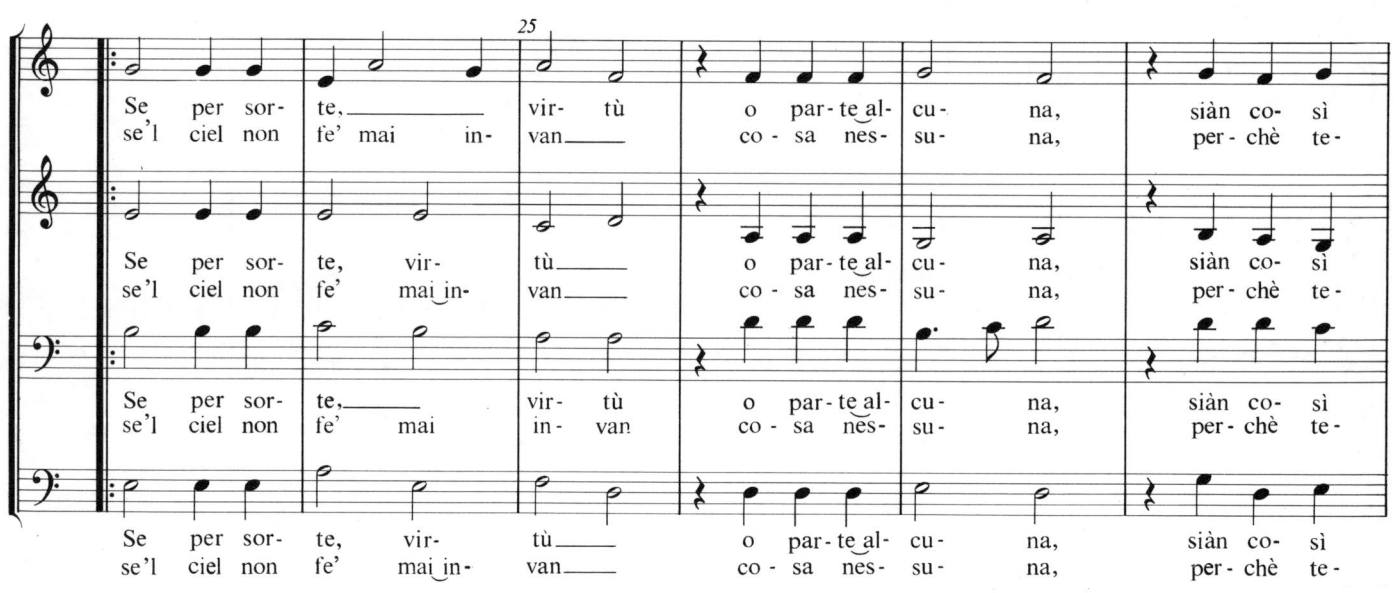

Gli è 'l ver che 'l prestar l'occhio a quello e questo
può dar gran sospezion di qualche errore;
ma l'eleggersi un còr degno e onesto
è gran piacere e non piccolo onore:
che un uomo senza amore
si può dir una pietra preziosa,
legata in piombo ascosa,
c'ha poca grazia e senz'util s'apprezza.

Questo nostro volere amar chi ci ama
è cosa bella, giusta e naturale,
perch'acquistar d'ingrato al mondo fama
è mancar d'esser uomo razionale;
ma voi fate ben male
non pensar ch'ancor voi giovani fusti,
perchè gli uomin giusti
hanno gran discrezion di giovinezza.

Godete, amanti, un poco oggi il vederci,
sperando un dì nel porto rinfrescarvi,
chè come amor c'insenga oggi dolerci,
così c'insegnerà poi contentarvi:
ma vogliàn ben pregarvi,
per ovviare al dir degl'indiscreti,
siate onesti e segreti,
ch'amor vuol fe', silenzio e gentilezza.

[23.] Canto della fortuna

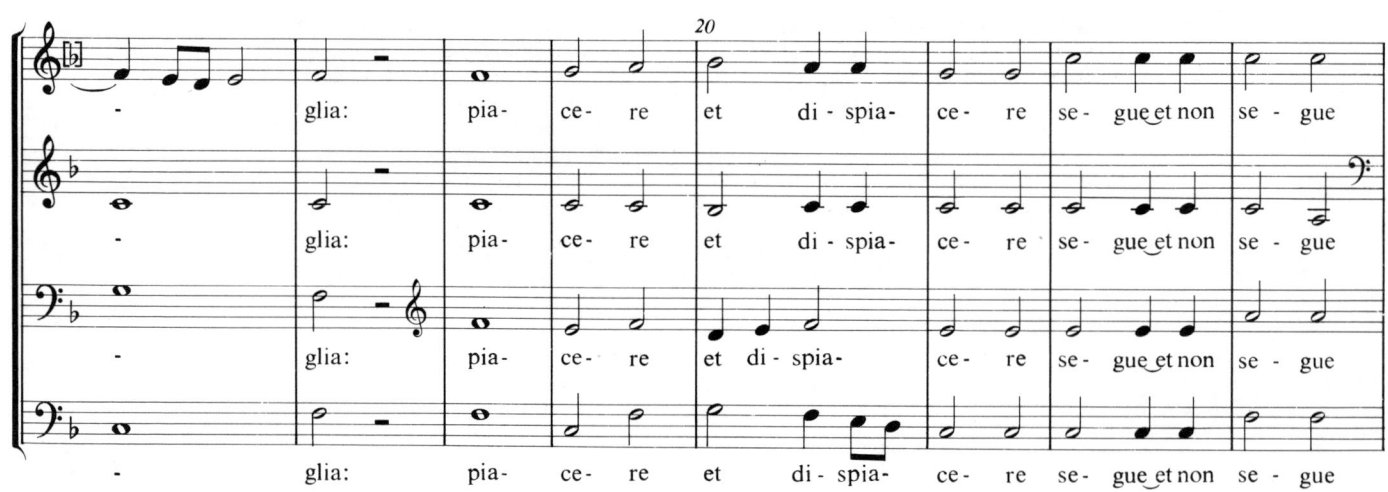

Questa è speranza a tutti e disperati,
questo è contento di ciaschun contento:
danna et salva e dannati;
fa el pianto riso e 'l riso fa lamento;
voltasi come el vento;
a chi dà toglie et a chi toglie rende:
et così ci baratta, guocha et vende.

Et perde te chi cercha altri che te,
et non può creder bene chi in altri crede:
subsidio, aiuto et fede
à chi felicemente ti possiede.
Ciaschuno or ti concede
l'honor del bene e 'l mal che qui si mostra:
et ogni tuo voler è voglia nostra.

[24.] Canto dei giudei

M. Alexander Coppinus
[Alessandro Coppini]

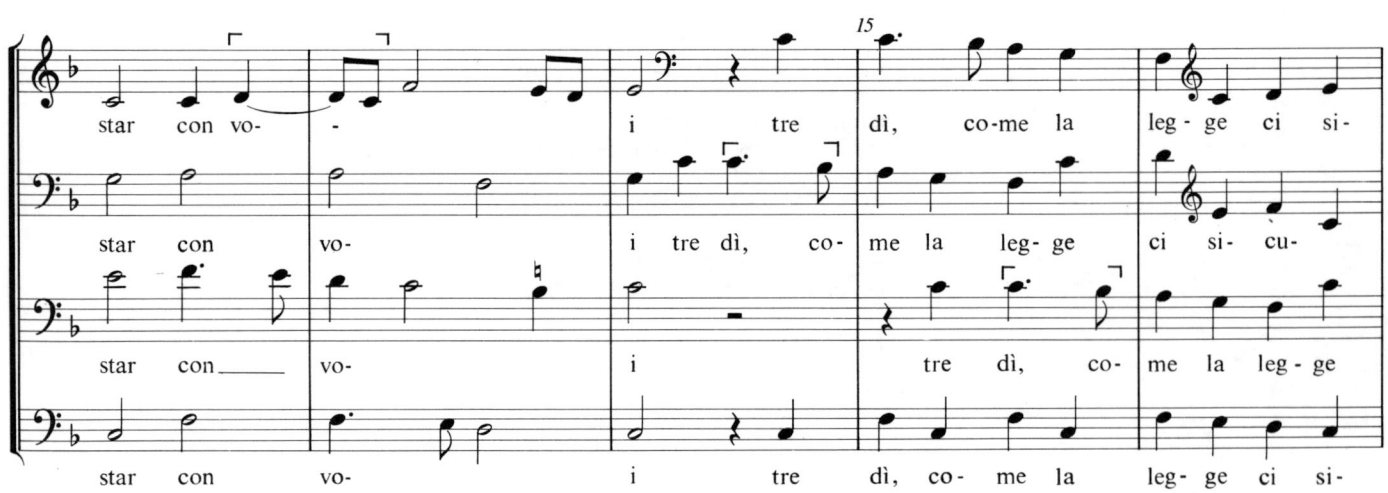

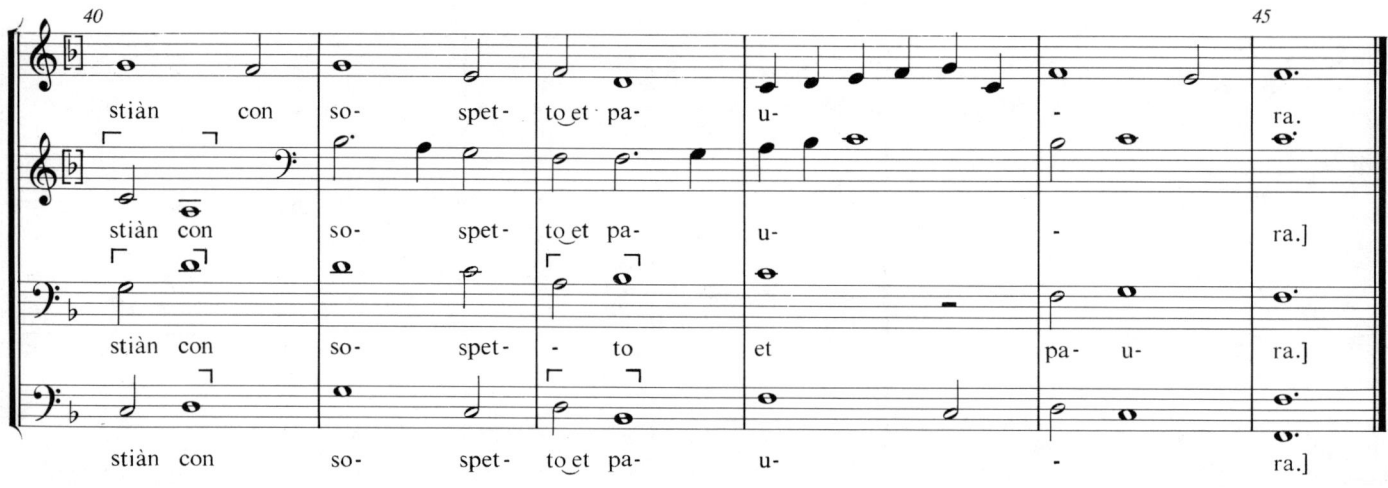

Già mille volte da noi achattasti
danar col pegnio in mano;
hor pochè l'arte me' di no' inparasti,
pover venuti siàno.
Ma parci un caso strano
che chi presta col pegnio
non porti el nostro segnio
et stie quanto e vuol drento a vostre mura.

No' sappiàn ben che non sol per guadagnio
con sicurtà prestate,
ma l'aiutare un povero conpagnio:
il che molto ben fate.
Et se voi guadagniate
è giusto et cosa honesta:
chè non fa mal chi presta;
ma chi achatta, fa mal dell'usura.

Non prestate a nessuno in sulla fede,
chè non ce n'è niente,
et sol ghabbato è quel che troppo crede:
po' con danno si pente.
Hor sia saggio et prudente
chi n'à richeza et stato:
ch'un ben, male aquistato,
se ne va in fummo presto et pocho dura.

Col pegnio è l'huom sicuro et non bisognia
semsali, trabalzi, et carte
per ricoprire; chè non s'à aver vergognia
di far ben la suo arte:
stiensi dunque da parte
scrochi, canbi et contratti;
fate horma' chiari e patti,
chè tutti poi alfin son pretta usura.

[25.] Canto delle ninfe

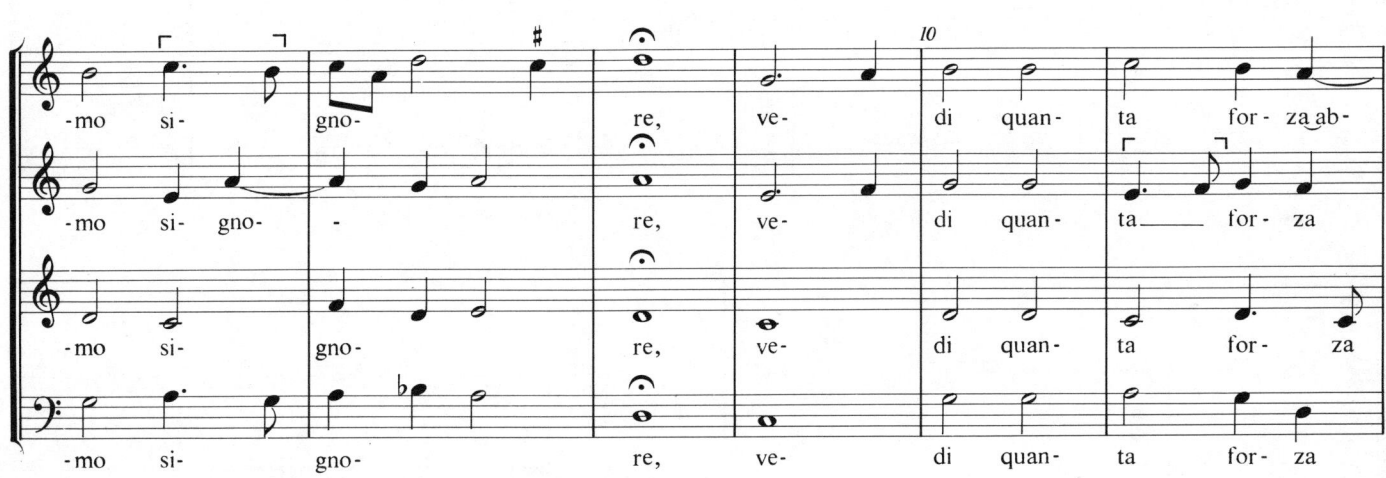
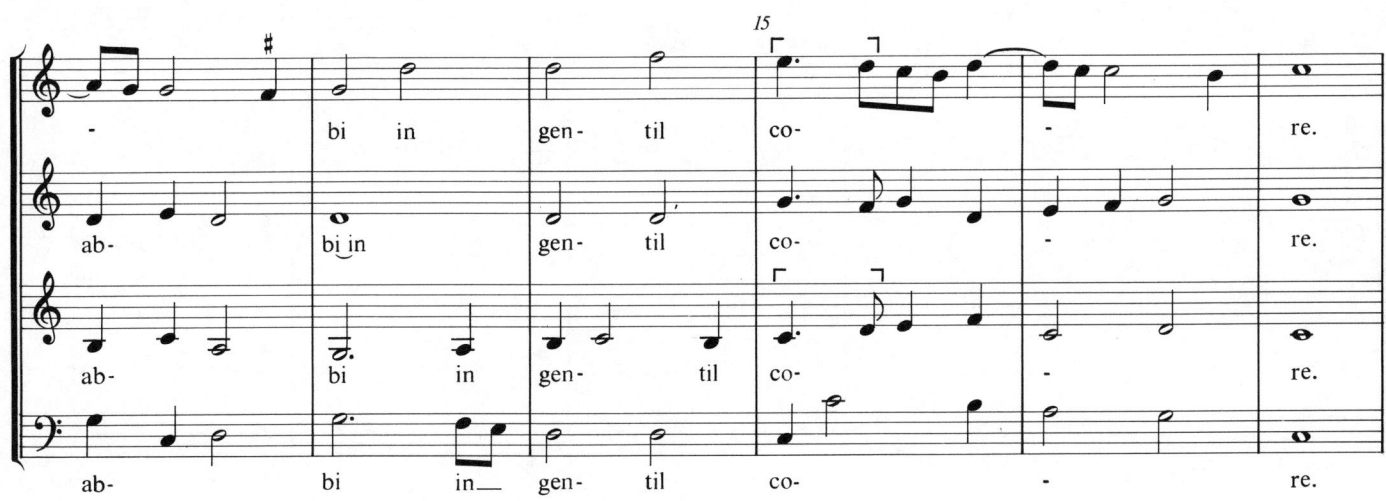

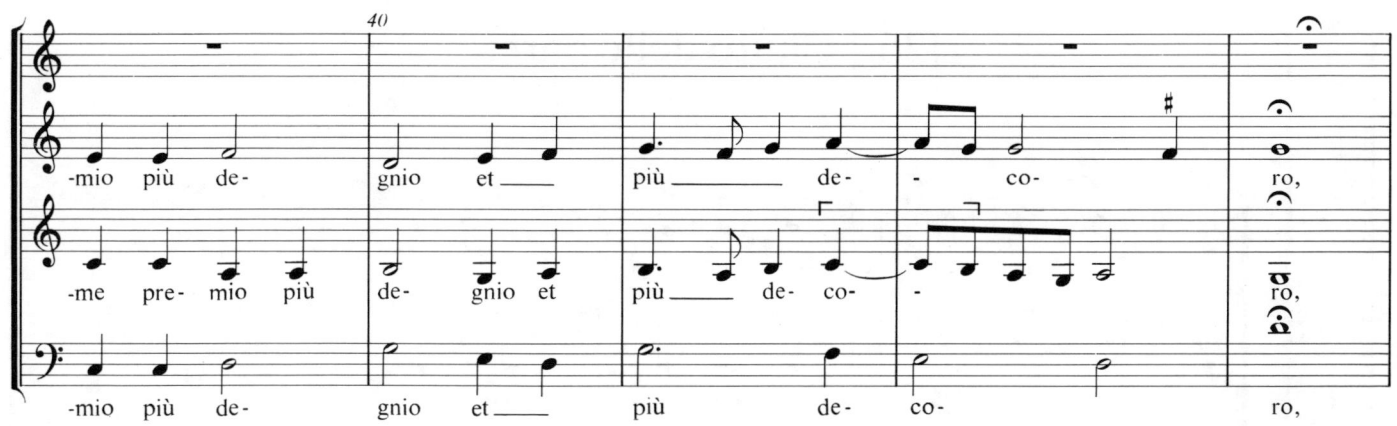

Cerere, in prima, dèa lieta et benignia,
suo flave spighe à messo;
le rose e 'l mirto suo ti dà Ciprignia;
Cibele el pino apresso,
l'irto et mesto cupresso
che piange ancor suo sorte inpia et malignia;
Minerva el frutto suo si mostra verde,
per mostrar che virtù mai valor perde.

Baccho l'uve suo varie, amene et mite,
signior, ti porge ognora,
e 'l pome onde tre dèe fer sì gran lite,
segue con queste anchora;
vedi Vertumno et Flora,
com'àn lor fronde et frutte insieme unite:
di disio vinte tutte et di par zelo,
ch'a virtuosi è sempre schiavo el cielo.

Questo è in premio, signore excelso, et in merto
della tuo gloria et fama;
questo mostra a ciaschun, che è saggio, aperto
quanto un buon signior s'ama;
el cielo e 'l mondo el chiama,
nè è mai di suo stato el giusto incerto;
ma sol tu ch'ognior n'ài la 'sperienza,
lieta bem puoi goderne oggi Fiorenza.

Guove, signore excelso, illustre et degnio,
che 'l suo favor t'à dato,
alzi el tuo sceptro et gloriose regnio;
Iunon regha el tuo stato;
sorte, fortuna et fato
sien sempre lieti al tuo famoso segnio;
et perchè sol può fama in gentil core,
rimbombi el ciel di tuo gloria et valore.

[26.] Canto delle parete

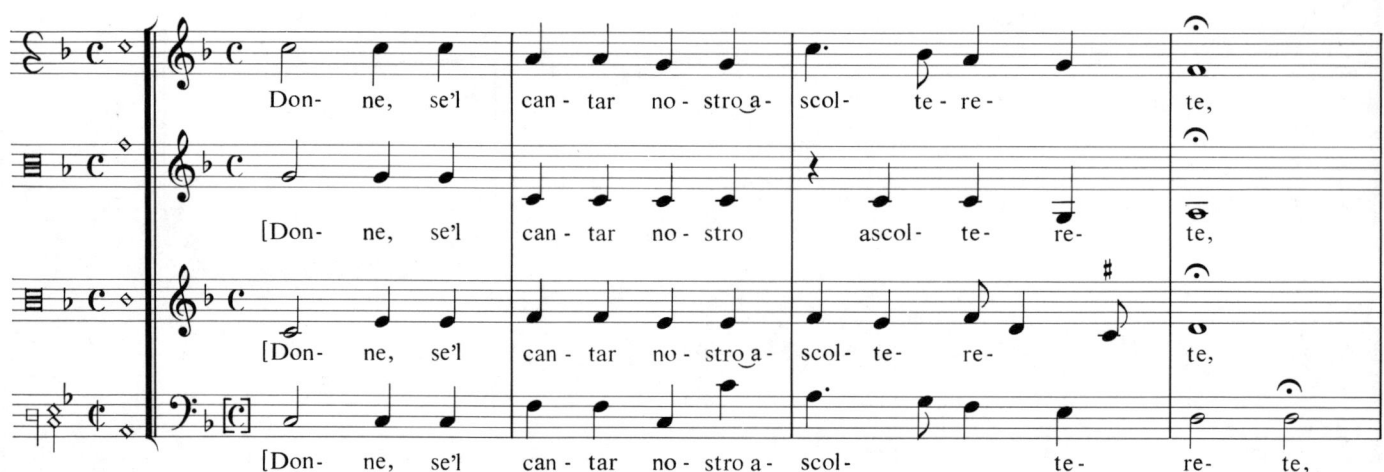

Per cantar, donne, ucce' di più ragione
d'aver sempre cerchate;
et qualche naturale et buon pincione
sopratutto ingabbiate:
ma, tenendolo in man, prima provate,
chè, se e' mozassi el verso,
in lui gutto invan perso el tenpo arete.

Quando si vede volteggiar l'uccello,
nè di calar fa segnio,
mettete, donne, allor mano al zinbello,
usando industria e 'ngegnio;
perchè tirare a tempo et con disegnio
esser quel si può dire,
c'ogni uccel fa venire sotto la rete.

Questi ucce', donne, c'hanno el capo rosso,
volentier caleranno;
ma quando egli ànno poi la rete adosso,
assai si scoteranno;
et quando chiusi nel ghabbion saranno,
perche e' prendin ristoro,
queste pannochie loro bechar darete.

Nel coprir ben consiste ogni inportanza
nel presente uccellare;
ma sopratutto abbiate per usanza
a ogni uccel tirare:
et non vi paia invano affatichare,
se nel calar vien solo,
ma tirando, al piuolo ben v'atterrete.

[27.] Canto di pastori bacchiatori di bassette

Baccio Florentino
[Bartolomeo Florentino]

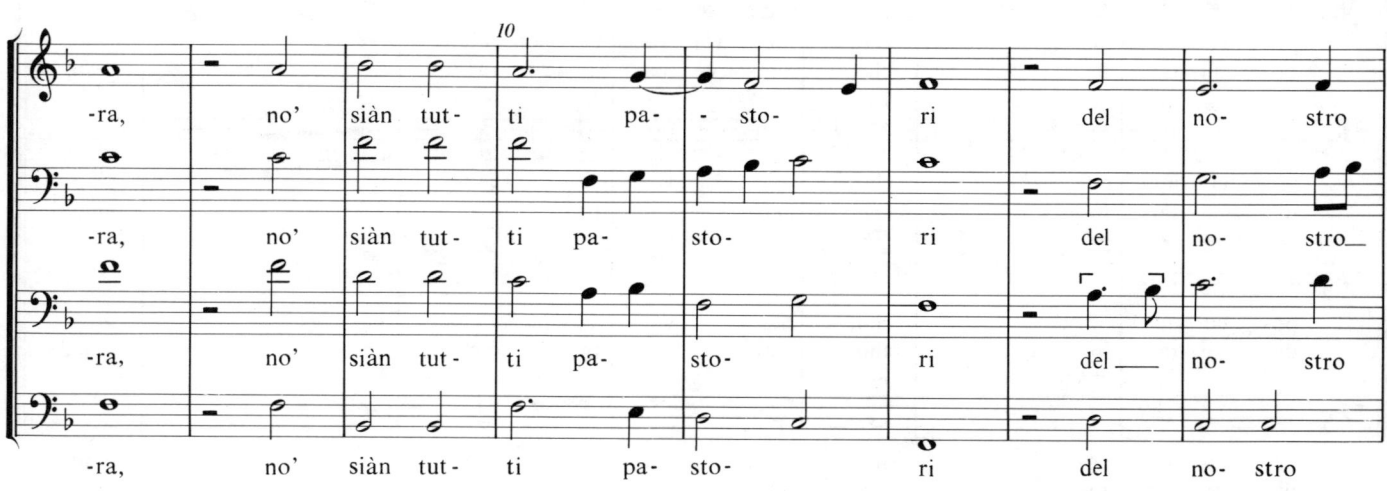
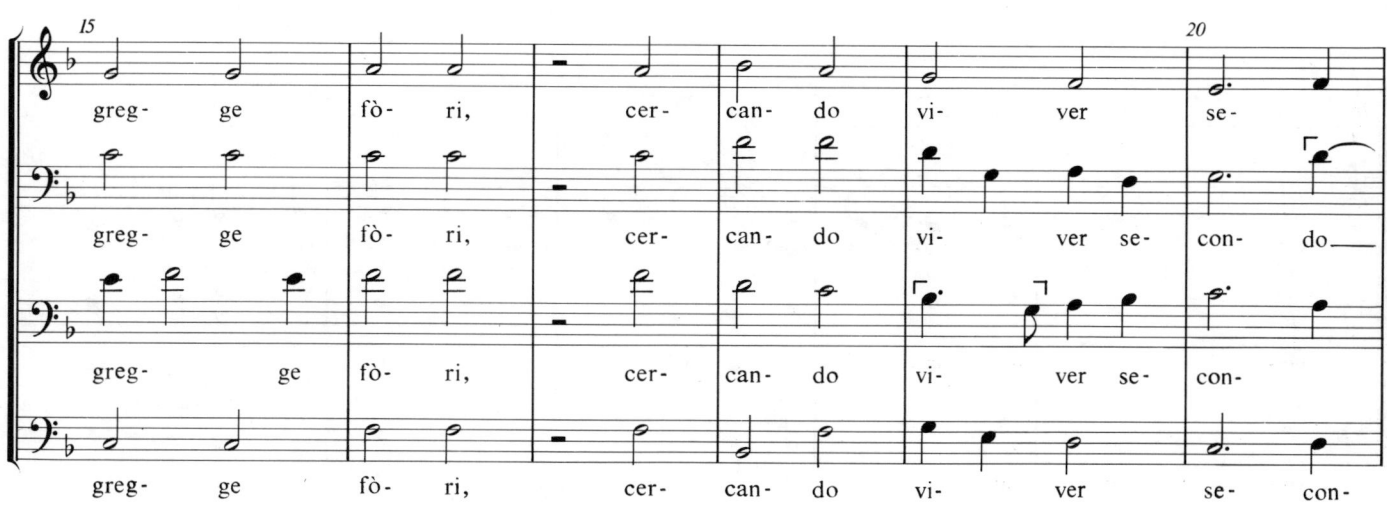

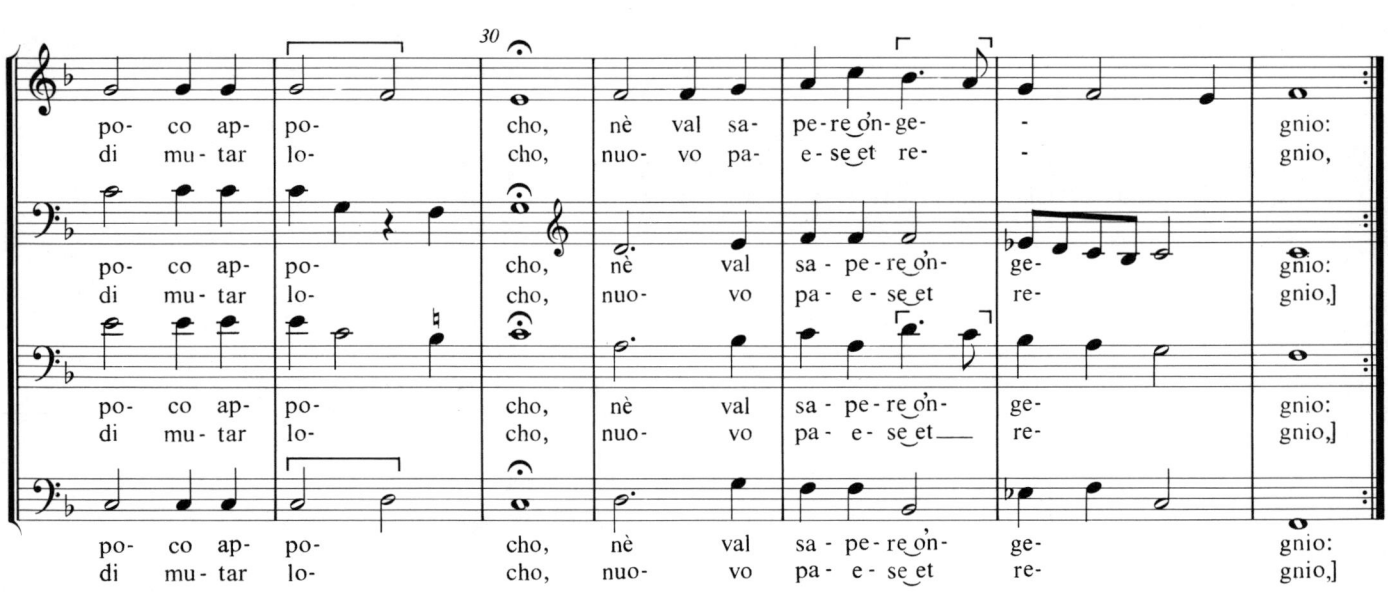

Credete voi però che el biancho faccia
bianchi tutti gl'agnegli:
se è ver ch'alla natura el vario piaccia,
gli farà neri et begli;
chi va cercando quegli,
punite per bachiare,
però che 'l voler dare
è stolta cosa, legge alla natura.

Se bachiassino a punto e contadini,
si potre' riparare;
ma perchè e' lo fanno anche e cittadini,
non si può rimediare;
lasciate rincarare
questa carne agnellina:
meglio è la vitellina,
et più propria a nutrir nostra natura.

Le ben nella vitella qualche bato,
che è buon bochon da ghioche;
quando gl'el tempo a quello comondato
ancio sin molti docti:
fassi di buoni (?)otti
anche colla vitella,
o di questa o di quella
stieri pure el monton di suo natura.

Perchè e nostri montoni son tutti neri,
grossi di bello aspetto,
ci è forza andarne per altri sentieri
a più dolze ricetto;
e 'l tòrne un piccoletto
da altri ci dispiace,
ch'a gl'intendenti piace
sempre la bestia grossa per natura.

Ghustate un po 'l sapor del nostro latte,
c'assai la pruova vale;
queste ricotte da noi testè fatte
non vi posson far male.
In questo carnasciale
ghoder con noi vi piaccia;
et con vergognia taccia
chi vuol trarre el monton di suo natura.

[28.] Canto di pescatori a lenza

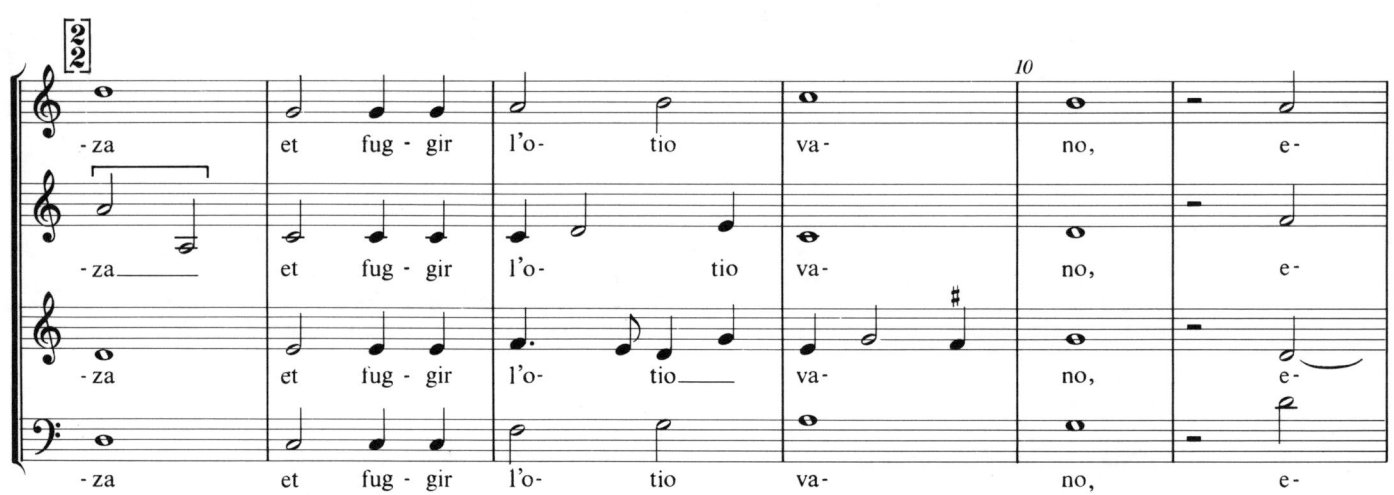

Quando si cuopre ellamo di buon'escha,
non si può fallir mai.
Però colui che 'n questo modo pescha
senpre aquistar vedrai;
et sopratutto delle lasche assai
si sogliono al bochon pigliare allenza.

Chi di tuffarsi è vagho et d'andar sotto,
gli avien quel che e' non crede:
chè quel che è più nell'arte sperto et dotto,
spesso affogar si vede.
Però in simil peschar non si pon fede,
se non pell'huom ch'à pocha intelligenza.

Chi 'l bucine al perchar talor prepara,
com'è l'ordine usato,
spesso sente tormento et doglia amara
pel frugar disperato;
et qualche volta gli è rotto o stiantato:
però non c'è al più bel peschar ch'allenza.

Qualche pescie villano al primo tratto
suol veloce fuggire;
però si vuol con maestrevole atto
quel coll'escha seguire,
perch'alla voglia sua lo fa venire
ogni buon peschator ch'à patienza.

[29.] Canto della pomata

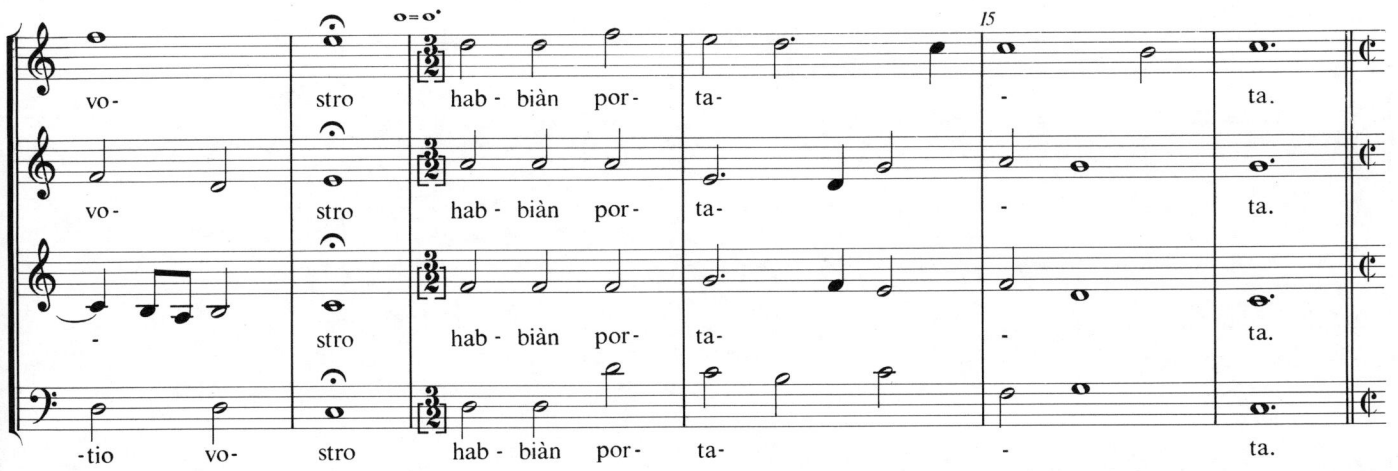

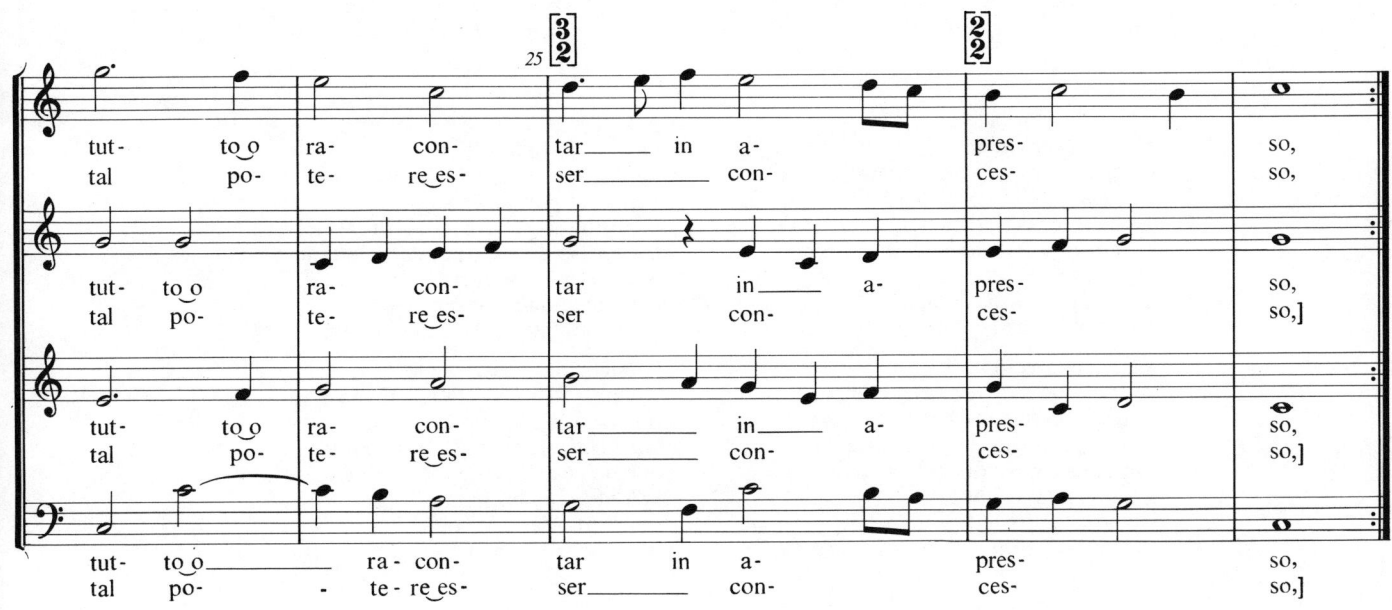

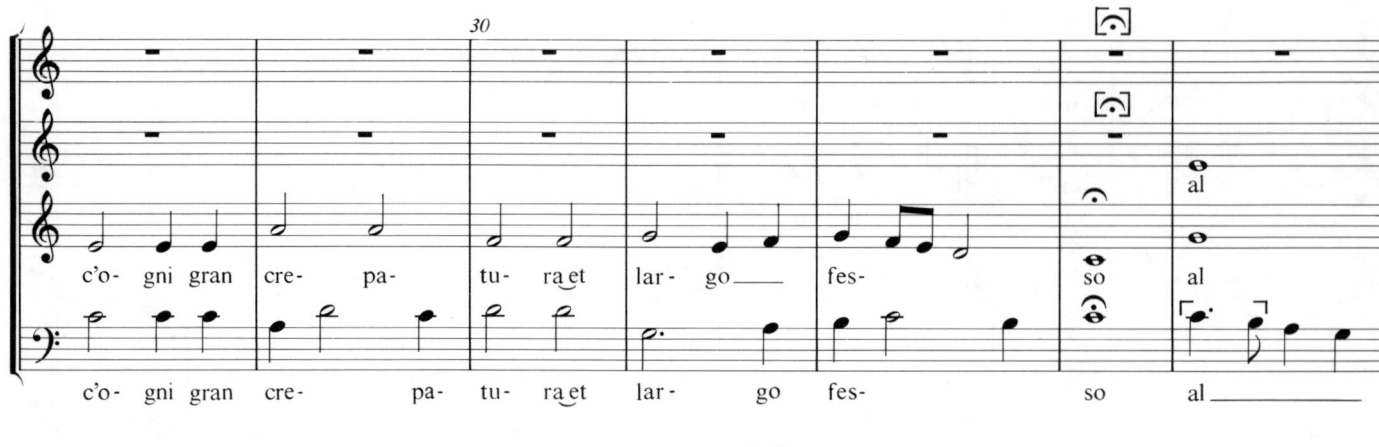

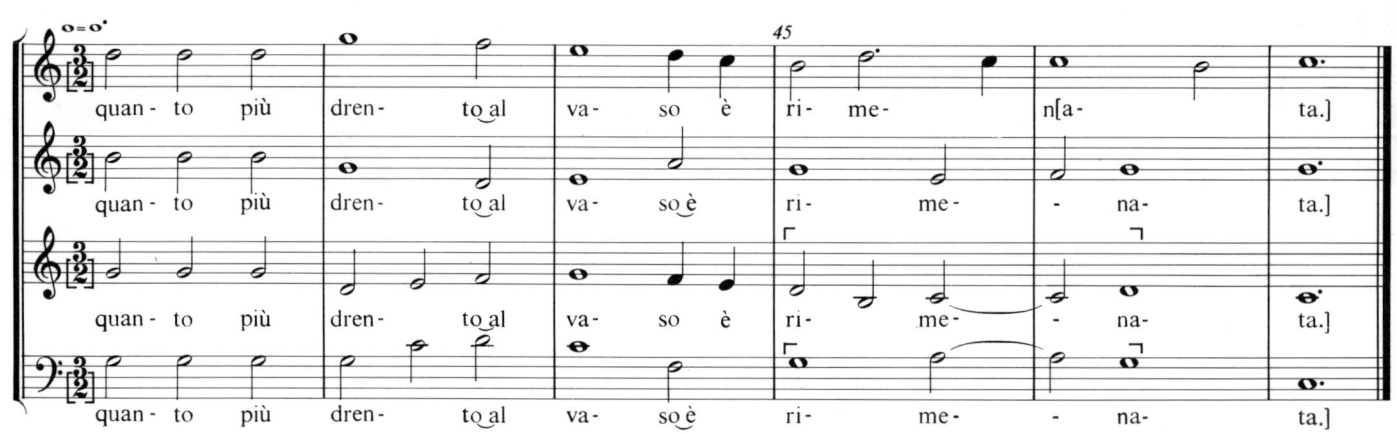

D'animal govinetto
si toglie el grasso a far questa unzione;
et quel che è più perfetto
si chava lor de lombi et dallo arnione,
et fassi insieme una incorporatione
con questo dolze pome:
et di qui proprio el nome
diriva et fa che l'è detta pomata.

Quando talvolta aviene
ch'u' nerbo ingrossa, incrudelisce et tira,
con questa unghasi bene
per fuggir doglia et placar la suo ira;
chè spesse volte di dolor sospira
chi non ha tal ricetta:
però molto perfetta
a quest'estremo, donne, è la pomata.

Ogni cosa villana,
unta con questa, par che si rassetti,
perchè la purgha et sana,
penetrando gl'humori ne' luoghi stretti;
ma spesso dato v'è più bossoletti
pien di falsa mestura:
abbiate adunque cura,
chè molti falsatori c'è di pomata.

Qualche donne esser suole
ch'enpiersi l'alberel vuol di suo mano,
nè mai di noi si duole,
che la misura fare allei lasciàno;
et benchè assai del nostro vi mettiàno,
volentier lo farèno
per contentarvi a pieno,
nè per altro portiàn questa pomata.

[30.] Canto dei poveri che accattano per carità

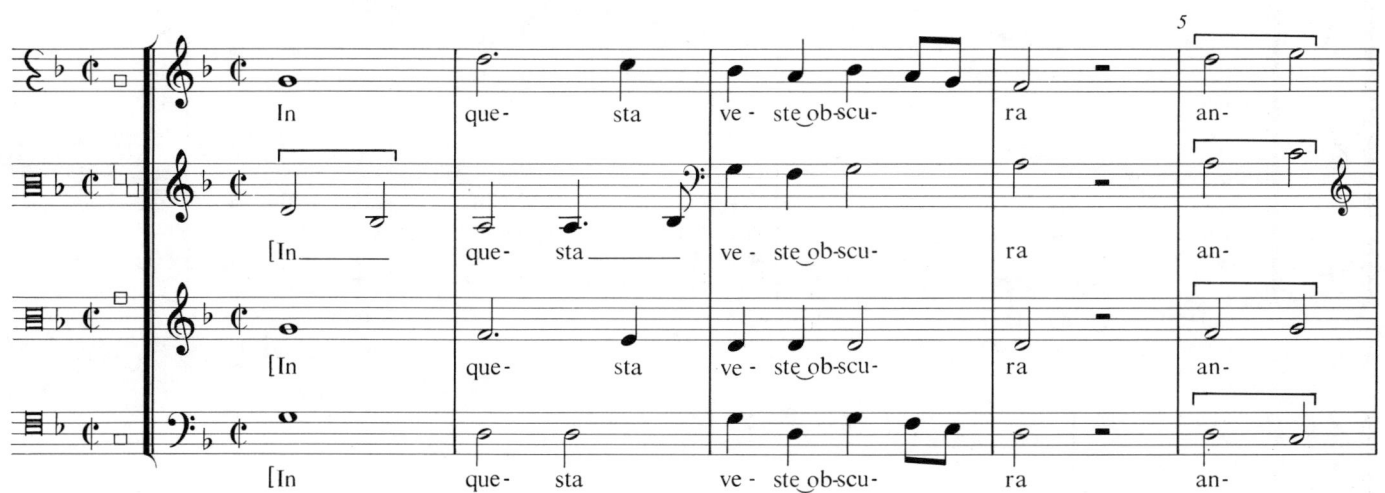
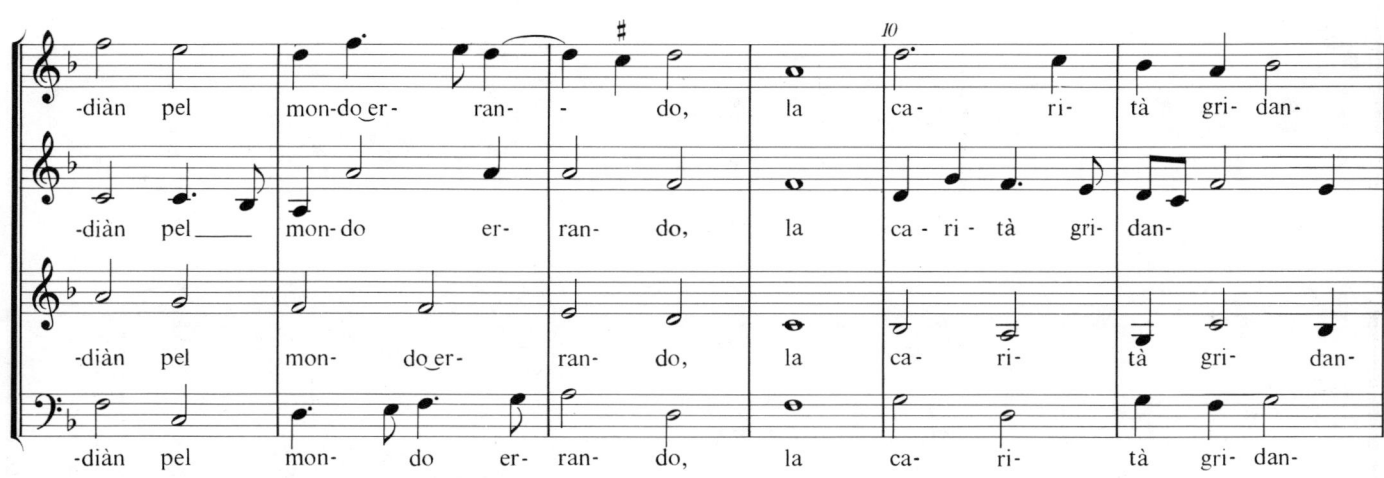

Uno amoroso stato
di gentileza et norma,
l'amante nello amato
la carità el trasforma;
colei ch'a far non dorma
che 'l bel tempo non dura.

Donne, se voi vedete,
che carità ci regge,
perchè sì crudel siete
a questa nostra legge;
chi ama, vede, et legge
quel ben che dà natura.

Questa rigida veste
quanti di fuor ne 'nghanna,
o donne, state deste,
sempre non piove manna;
tale altri spesso danna
che di se à paura.

Dunque, donne, pensate
d'amar sempre con fede,
accochè poi troviate
dal cielo grata merzede;
chi mette in fallo el piede
fa poi la faccia oscura.

[31.] Canto della prudenza

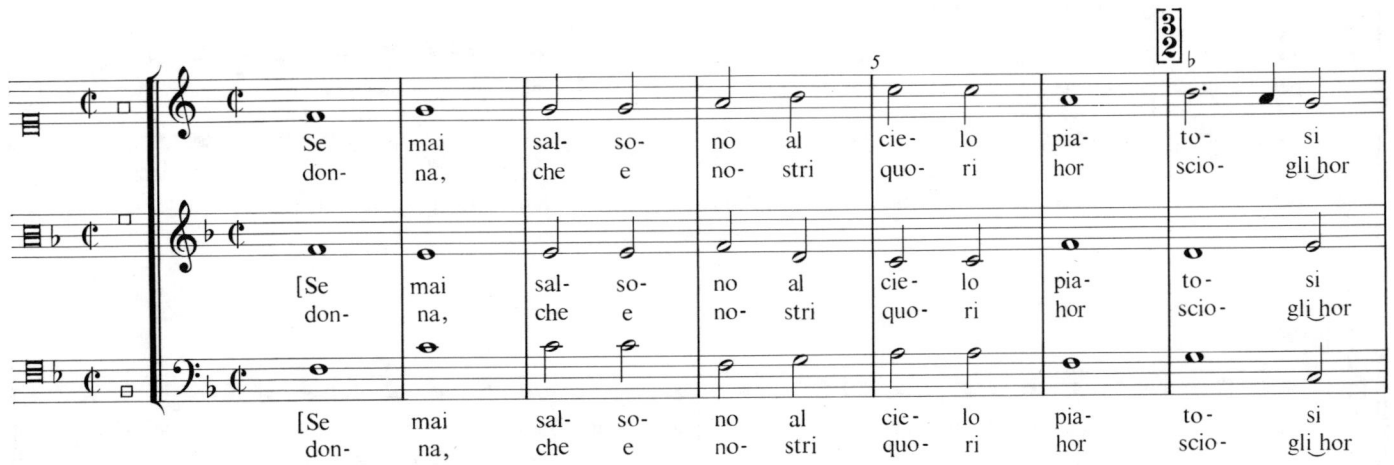
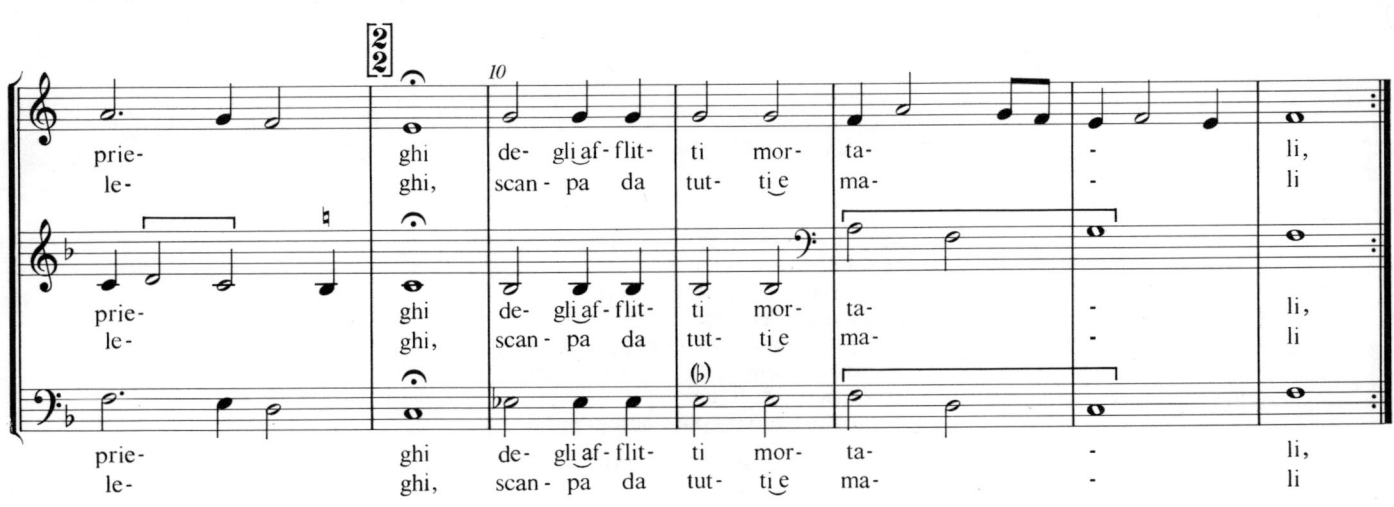
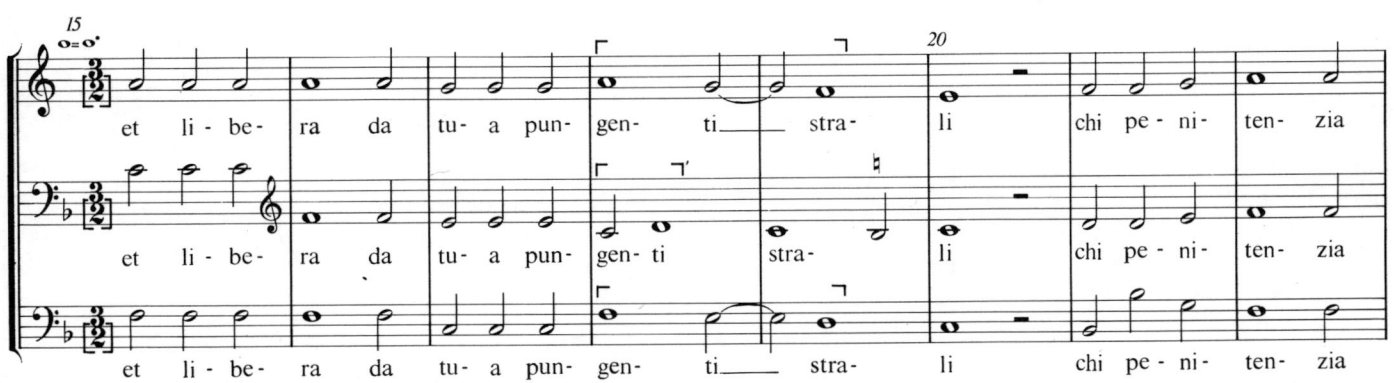

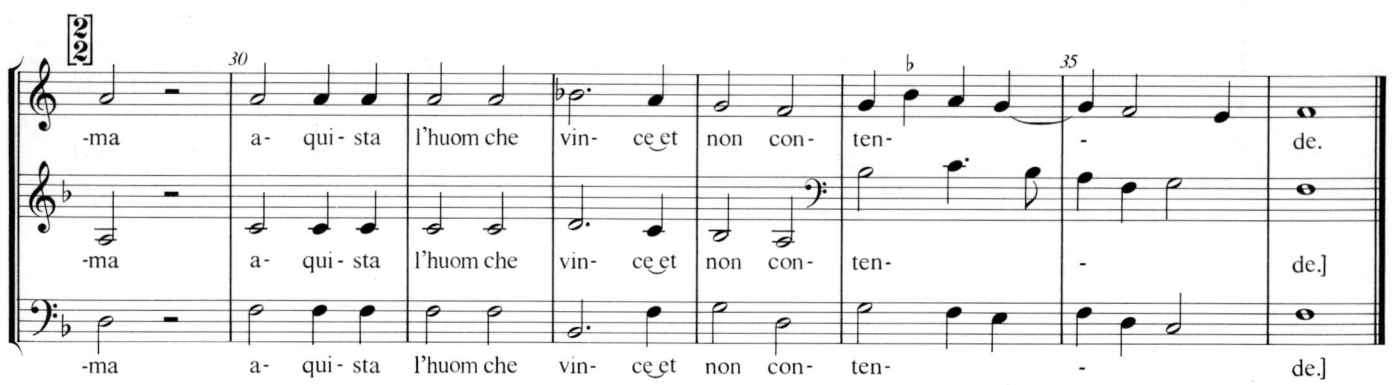

Se sè dal dolze nodo mai si scioglie
un sol di nostra gente:
allor satia, madonna, le tuo voglie
et la tua aspra mente;
et di piatà per noi sien tutte spente
le forze, et vòlte tutte a' nostri danni;
et con pene et affanni
ci pon dove tuo ira poi s'accende.

O voi che in tanti affanni ci vedete
per non l'aver seguita;
et tutti e nostri danni or conosciete
et la misera vita:
pregate questa donna alta et gradita
che vi riceva fra suo gente eletta:
prudenza ogniuno accetta
che el chammin ver di nostra vita prende.

[32.] Trionfo della prudenza

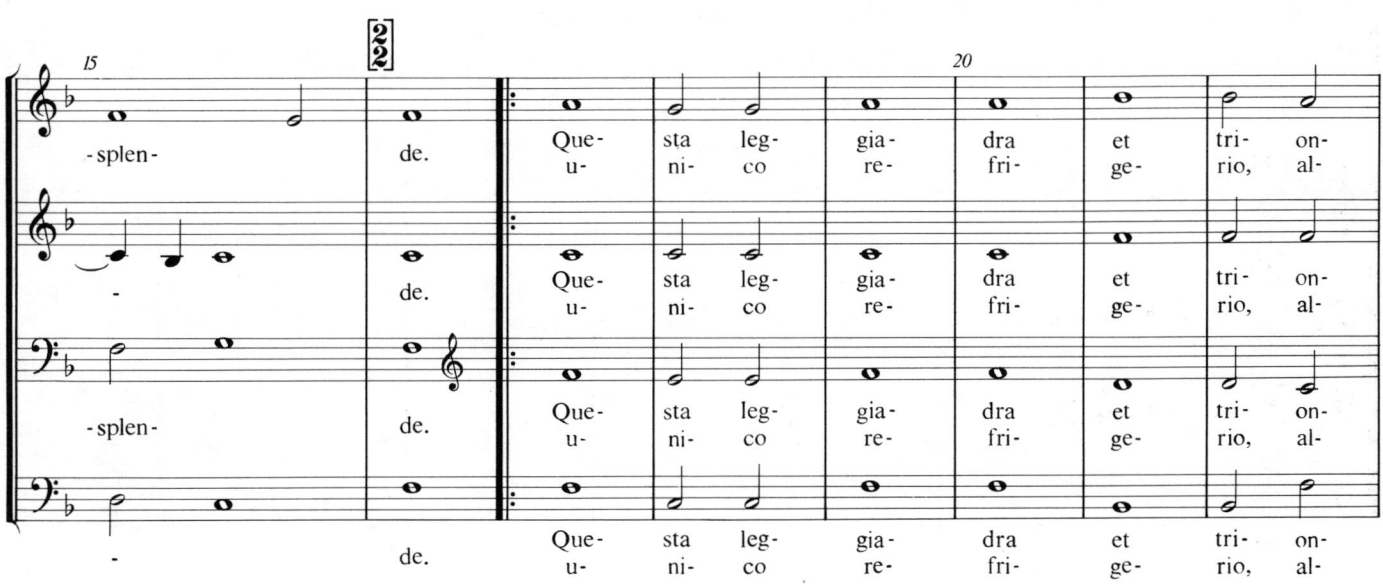

L'una è speranza; et l'altra, ch'a un laccio
medesmo el collo piega,
paura è detta, che nel core un diaccio
sì freddo a tutti lega
c'ogni riposo, ogni quiete niega
a chi ne' suo' legami si ritruova;
et pocho a costor giova
cerchar piatà dove è chi sempre offende.

Hor l'una et l'altra di lor morta iace
sotto e piè di costei
c'ha posto el mondo in sempiterna pace,
pochè à spenta colei
che sotto el duro freno huomini et dèi
insieme acolti a un giogo tenea;
nè inpetrar si potea
merzè dov'ogni crudeltà s'asconde.

Chi cercha dopo morte un'altra vita
più felice trovare,
et l'alma, pochè fia da noi partita
viepiù che in vita ornare,
questa sol donna ci può liberare
da morte et porre in più felice stato,
et fare ogniun beato
che sol suo scudo si quopre et difende.

[33.] Trionfo dei quattro tempi dell'anno

Tutta coperta d'erbe, fronde et fiori
vedete primavera
spargere al fresco vento mille odori;
scherzare a coppia et più non gire a stiera
sotto la verde fronde
ogni uccello, ogni fèra
pel caldo humor che nelle vene abbonde.

Nuda la state, et dal sol cotta et tinta,
a costei viene a spalle,
di varie spighe el capo ornata et cinta;
et colla falce le biade già gialle
seghando va per tutto,
fin ch'ogni poggio et valle
el fior conduce al disiato frutto.

Declina l'anno et l'autumno priva
gli arbor de' suo' honori,
et sotto e pie calchando l'uva stiva,
tutto giocondo el vin fa stizar fuori;
et sotto el gioghо preme,
arando, e franchi tori,
et per l'altro anno in terra asconde el seme.

Squallido, rotto da pioggia et da vento,
grandine, diaccio et neve,
seguita el vechio verno pigro et lento,
a se medesmo dispettoso et grieve;
chinando atterra el volto,
onde con segue in breve
degli altri tenpi el sudor fie sepolto.

Ma lasso! donne, quanto è peggior sorte
la nostra che la loro:
l'anno ritorna et non gli nuoce morte;
a noi non val saper, belleza o oro:
adunque in govineza
conosciàno el tesoro
che presto ci fie tolto da vechieza.

[34.] Canto dei romiti

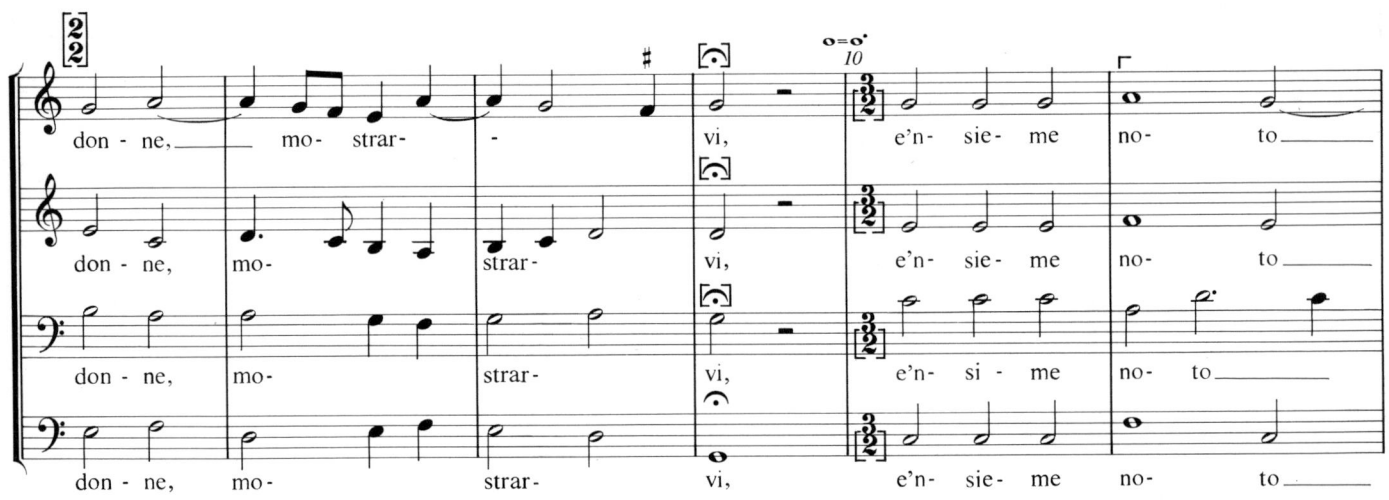
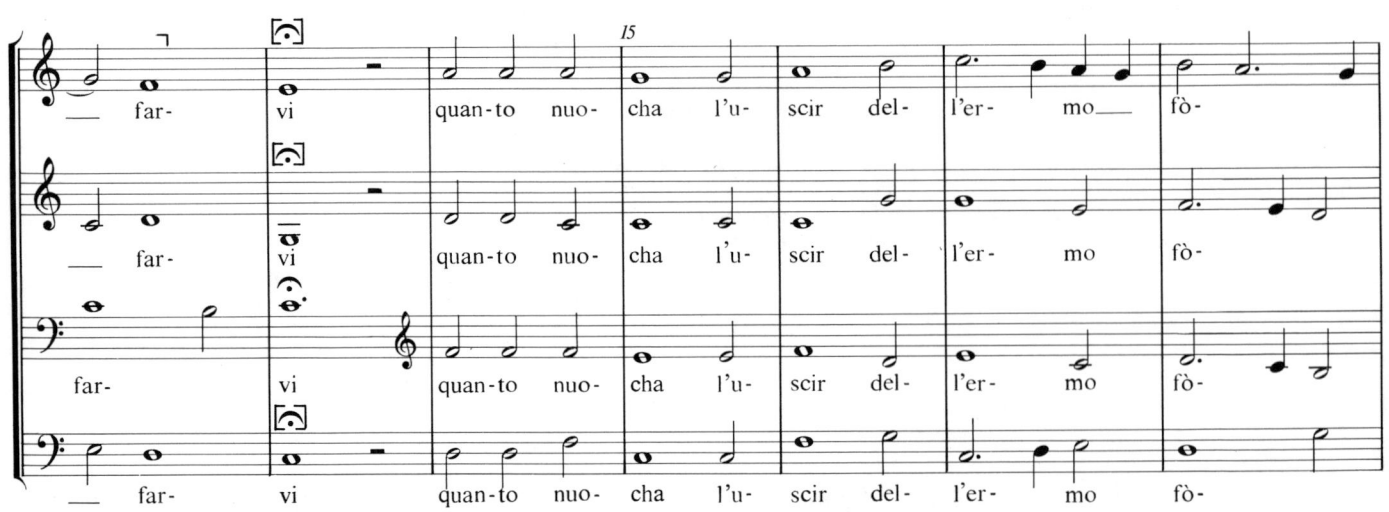

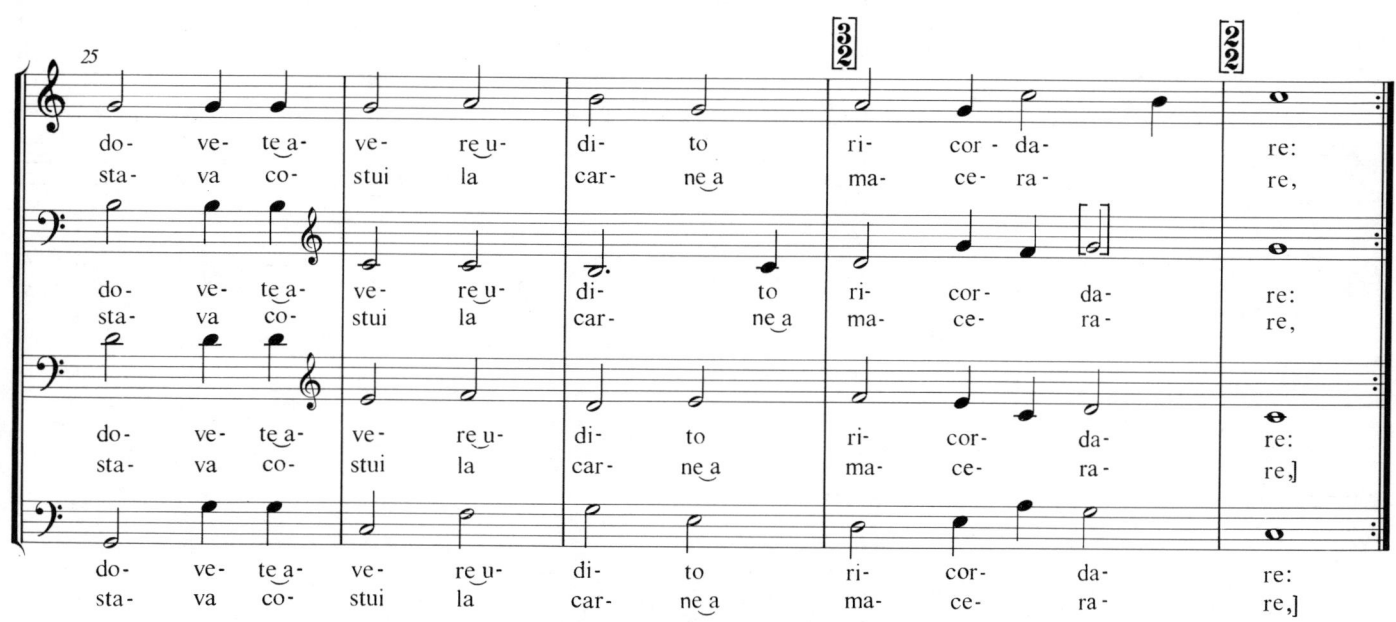

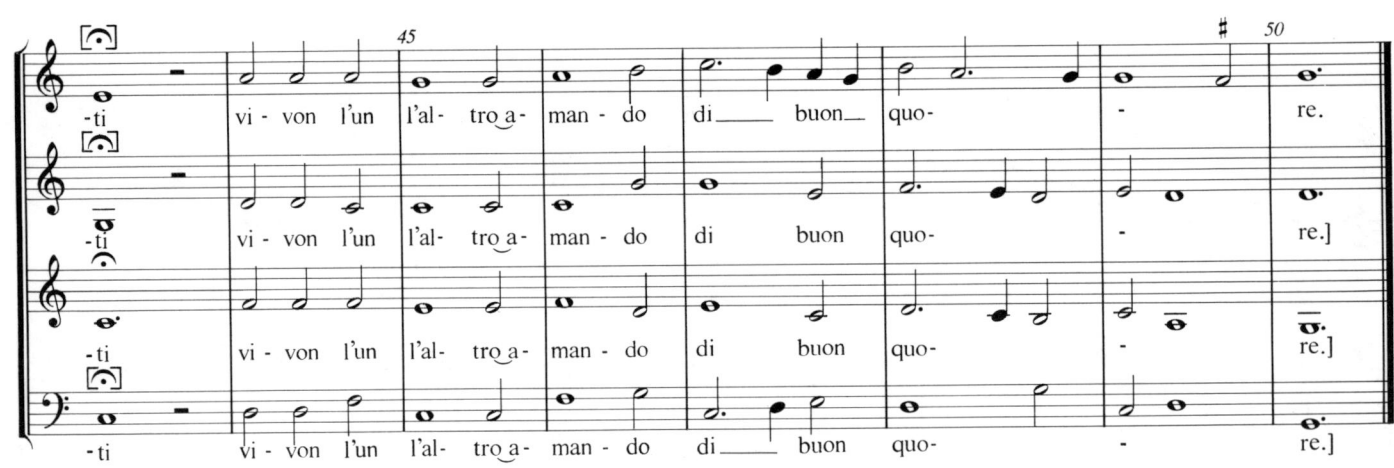

Hor sendo qua venuto
di nuovo a sodisfare un boto loro,
gli venne oggi veduto
una che siede nel bel vostro coro:
et perchè al mondo è soro,
non crede hor ch'altro paradiso sia,
se non dove lei stia;
et più cerchar non vuol d'altro signore.

Ecco poi come fa
chi non è uso a veder donne in viso;
ch'a voi prigion si dà
al primo sgardo et lascia el paradiso.
Costui stato è diviso
già tanto tempo dal consortio humano;
hora, in un punto, insano
diventa et cade in tanto acerbo errore.

Donne, prender vogliate
c'ò ch'e' vi dà, che so vi troverrete
più in man che non pensate,
chè e' non à pocho, come voi credete:
poi collui danzerete,
nè indarno e passi vi parrà aver persi;
et noi altri conversi
seguirèn l'orme del nostro maggiore.

[35.] Canto de' savi

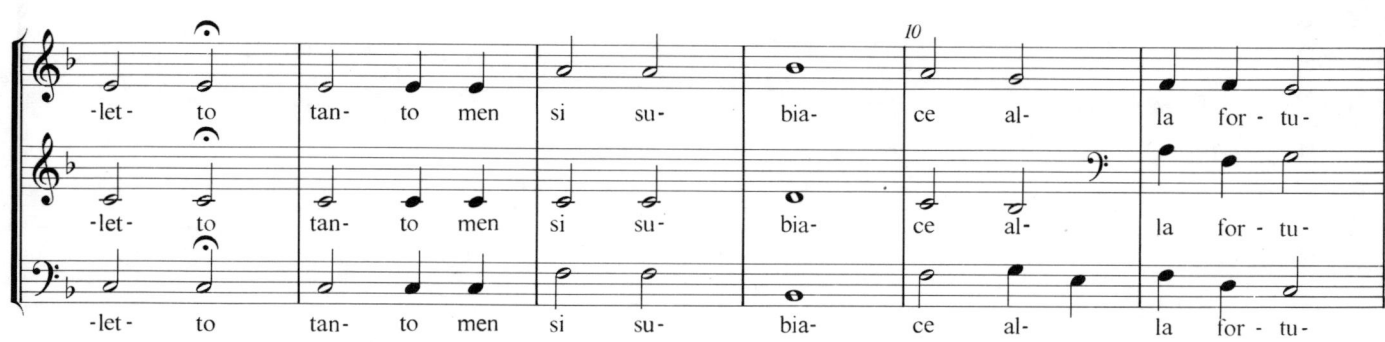
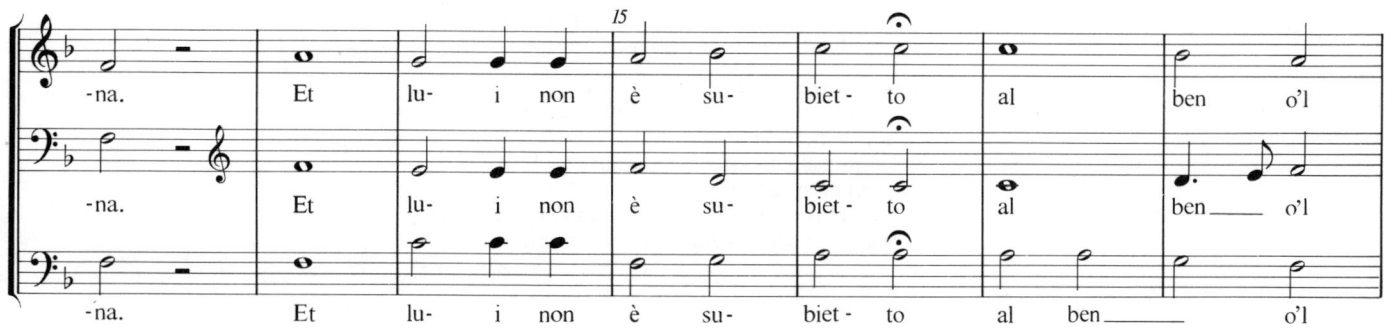
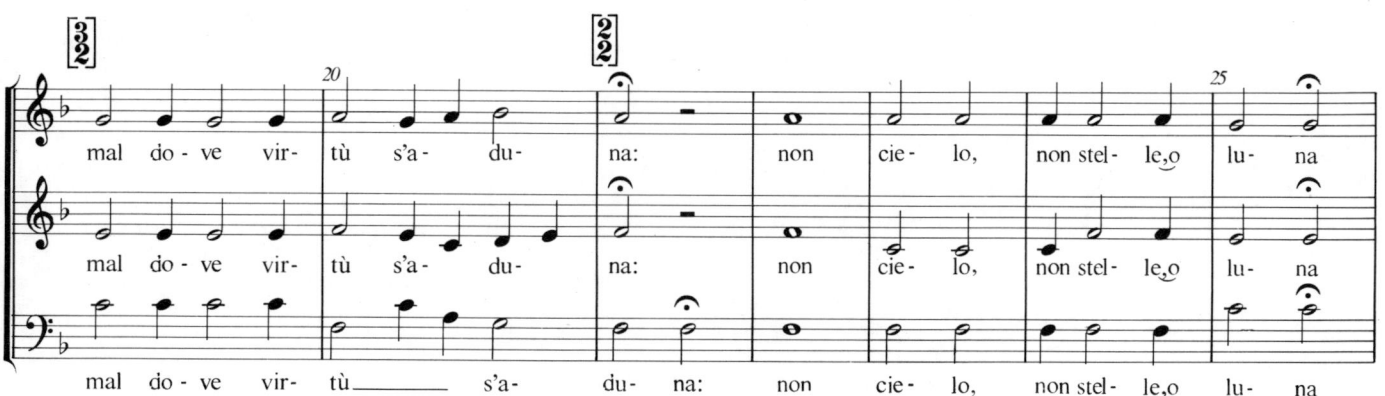

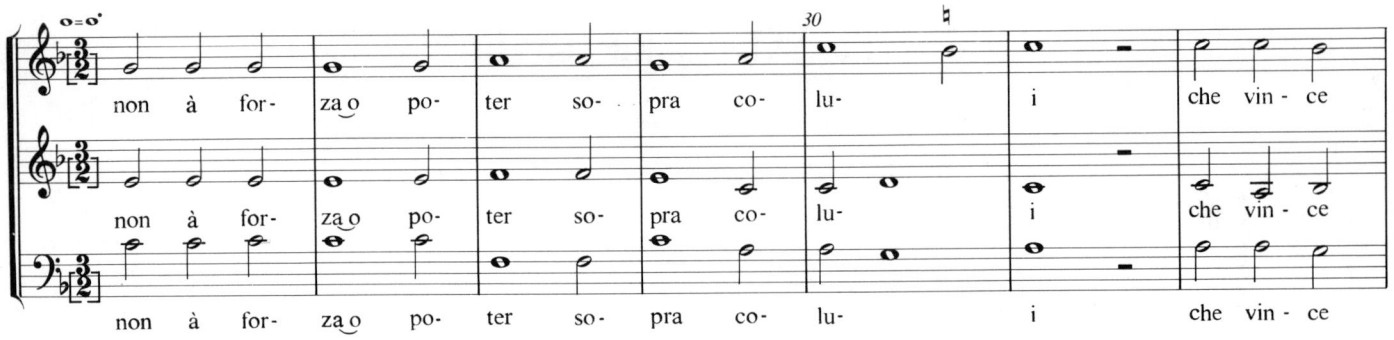

Felici tempi, miseri e 'nfelici,
el savio sanza sturbo gli conporta:
retti et justi iudìci
usa nel bene, e 'l mal non lo trasporta;
et ogni cosa porta
seco, sprezando gemme, oro et argento,
et sol del suo saper riman contento.

Et tante volte el còr parte da noi
quante in vari pensier di fuor trascorre;
torna quando tu vuoi
et quel che tu vuoi tu, nessun può tòrre:
fortuna o ciel disporre
non può del tuo voler più che tu voglia:
ma fa' che 'l tuo volere è la lor voglia.

[36.] Trionfo delle tre parche

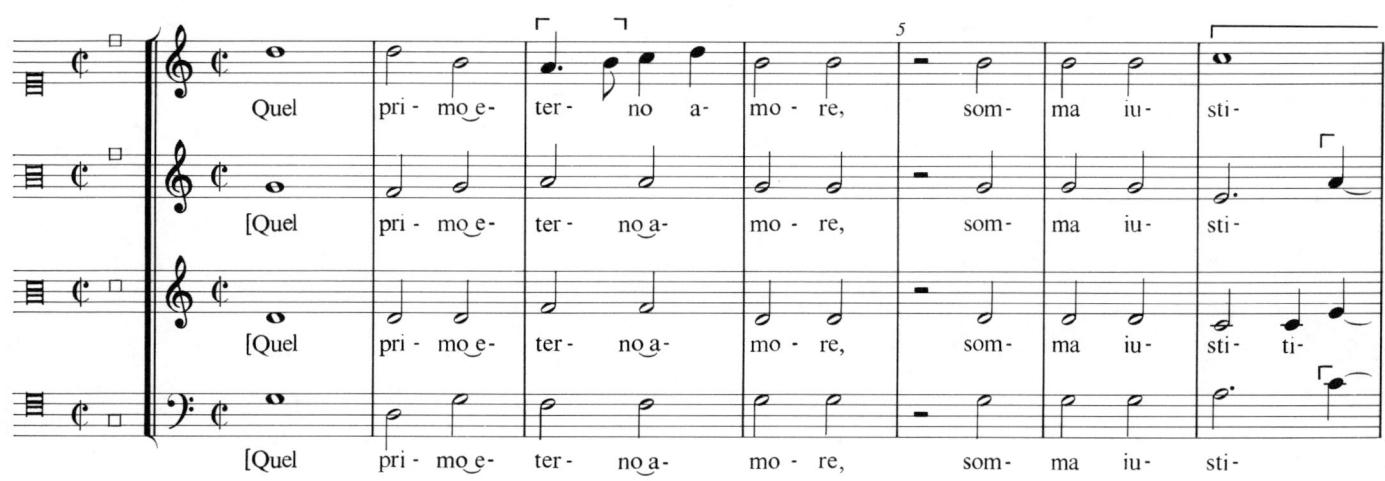
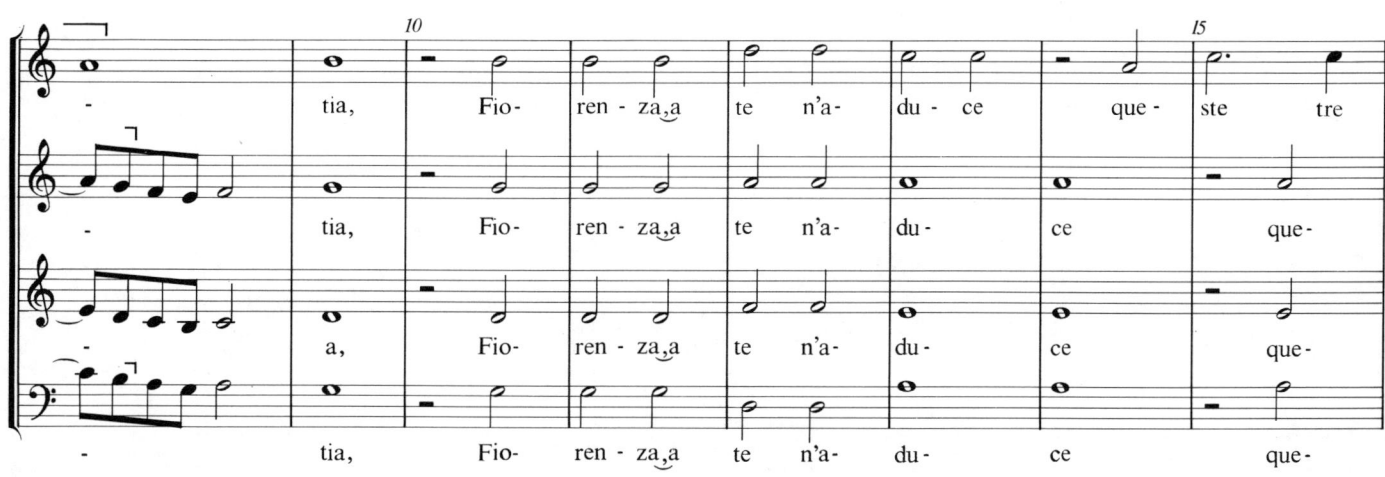

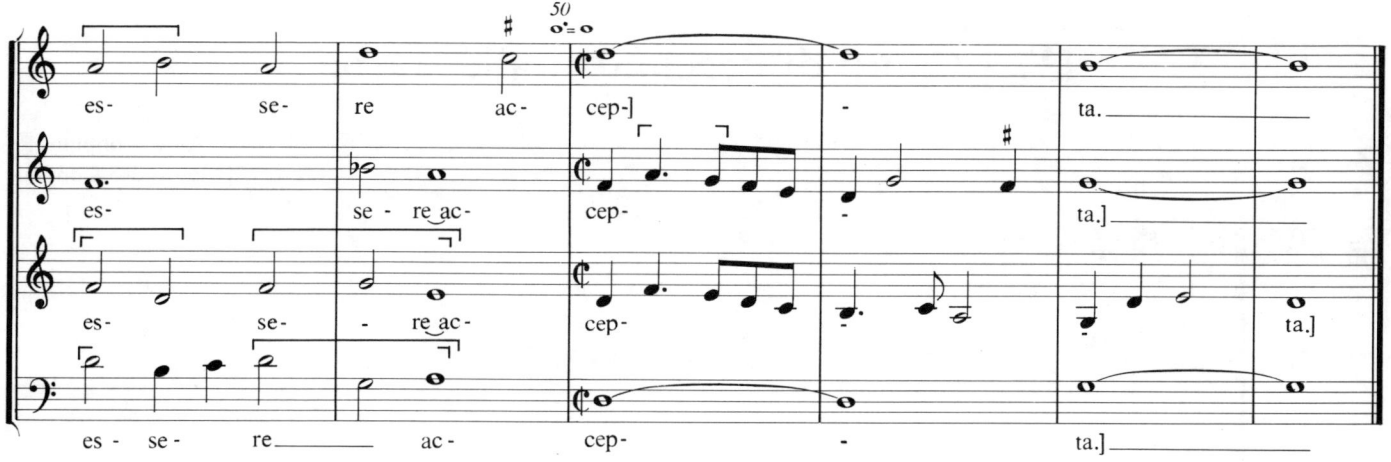

Quando fu posto in terra ordin e amore
dall'inmensa bontà,
perch'ogni cosa nasce, vive et mòre,
nacquon costoro della necessità:
l'una dà vita al core,
l'altra 'l viver mantiene,
l'ultima è fine a nostro danno o bene.

Però Lachesi el lino a rocha pone,
che ci dà vita et corte;
Cloto, filando, dà la perfectione;
Atropos troncha 'l filo quando vuol morte;
et così ferma et forte
è queste legge, et fia,
che tutto nascha et viva et morto sia.

Noi, con l'età che el cielo benignio presta,
vinciàn fortuna adversa;
la biancha pueritia aspira a questa,
senectù negra piange averla persa:
horsù, tutti, con questa
honoriàn Cloto nostra,
che più felice stato et ben ci mostra.

Et come el mezo tien della natura,
del principio et del fine,
così è ancora in noi quella alma pura
che presto inpetra le gratie divine,
et questa età futura,
per virtù, et presente;
ch'al passato e 'l venir pensa e 'l pendente.

[37.] Canto di uccellatori alle starne

Alex. Coppinus
[Alessandro Coppini]

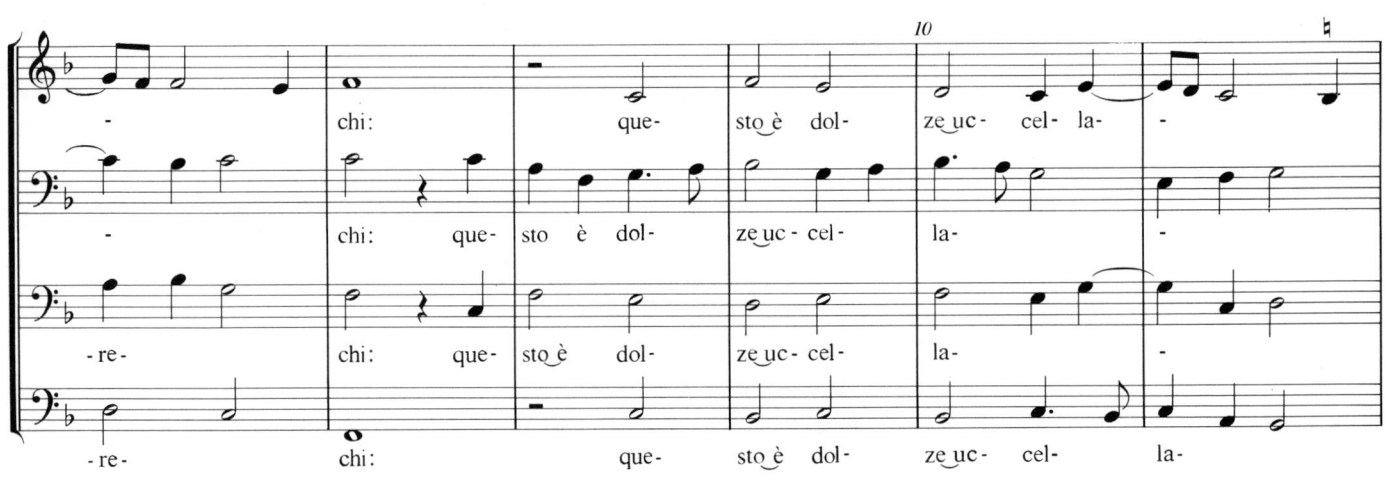
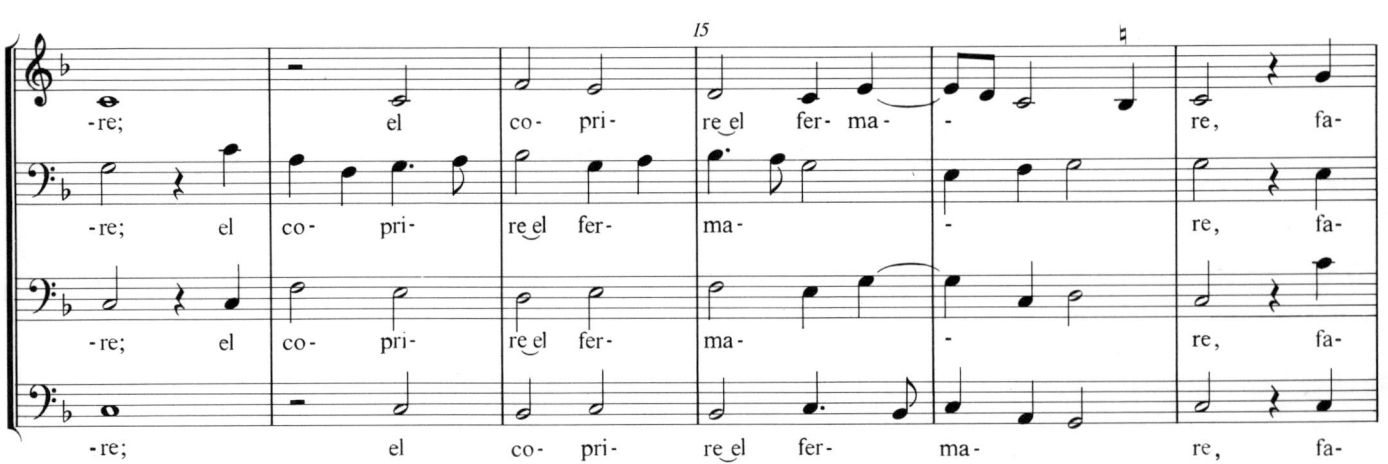

Sopratutto bisognia che e brachetti
abbin gra' naso grosso, et bella testa,
che son segni perfetti:
lascia poi fare alloro alla foresta;
chè se fien brachi eletti
inanzi e 'ndrieto senpre con assalti
trascorron per le stoppie a lanci et salti.

E' vogliono esser maschi et mantovani,
c'hanno maggiore ingegnio di natura
che vostri 'taliani;
ma d'una cosa sola abbiate cura,
et questo è de' pantani,
et chi fa chaccia più vantaggio a' brachi,
quanto più quopre, par mancho si strachi.

Àn questi brachi un'altra gentileza,
che com'e' senton la fera da presso,
dimostrando allegreza,
menon la coda più forte et più spesso;
ma quel ch'oggi s'apreza
che destri si rivoltin sottosopra
ciaschuna fera accochè me' si squopra.

[38.] Canto di uomini vecchi allegri e goditori

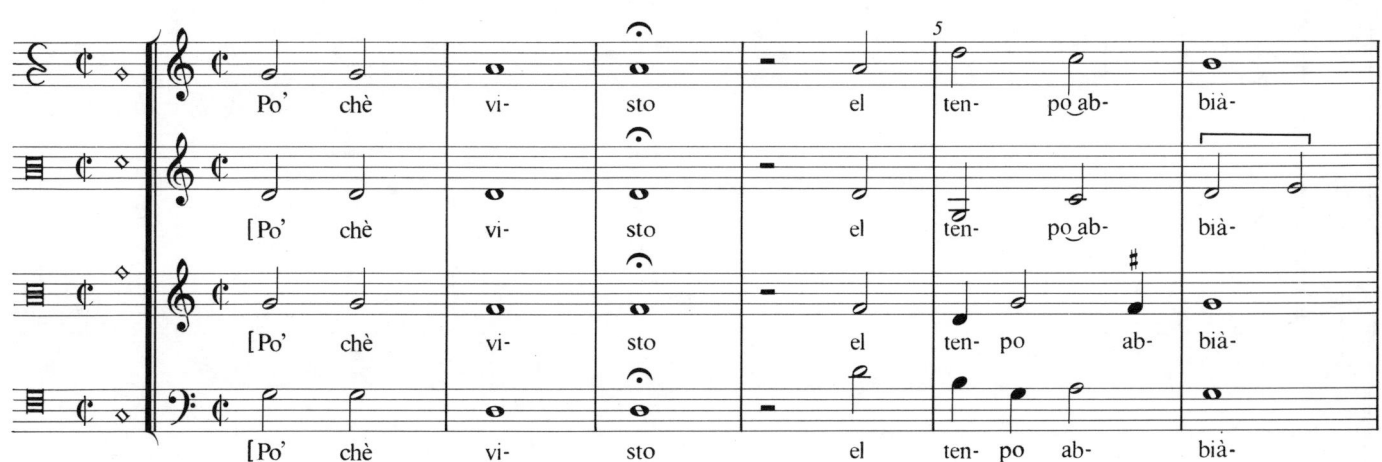

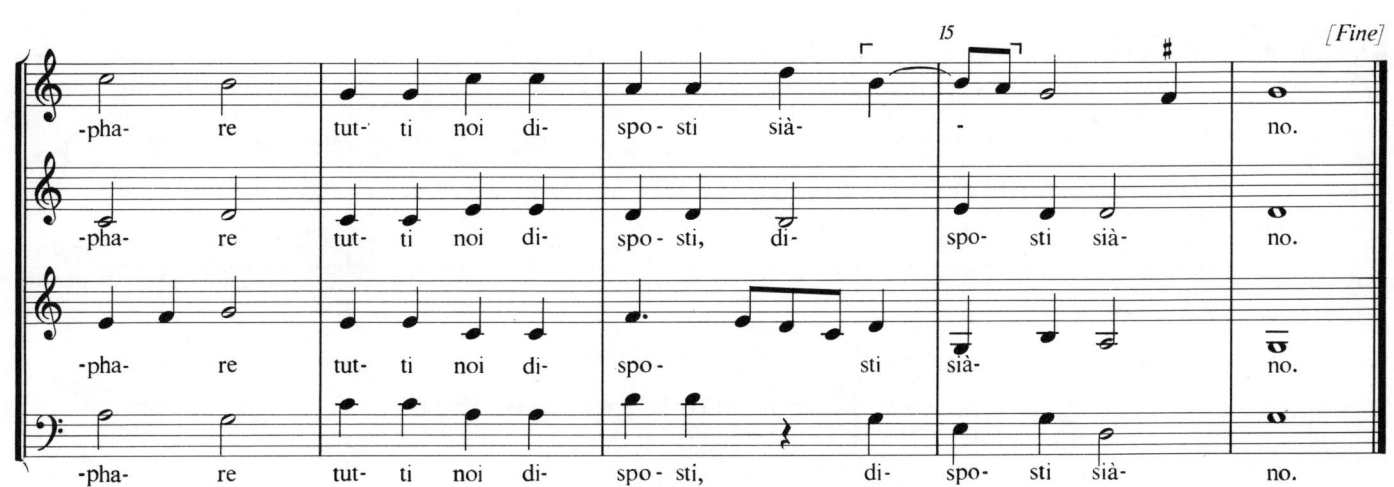

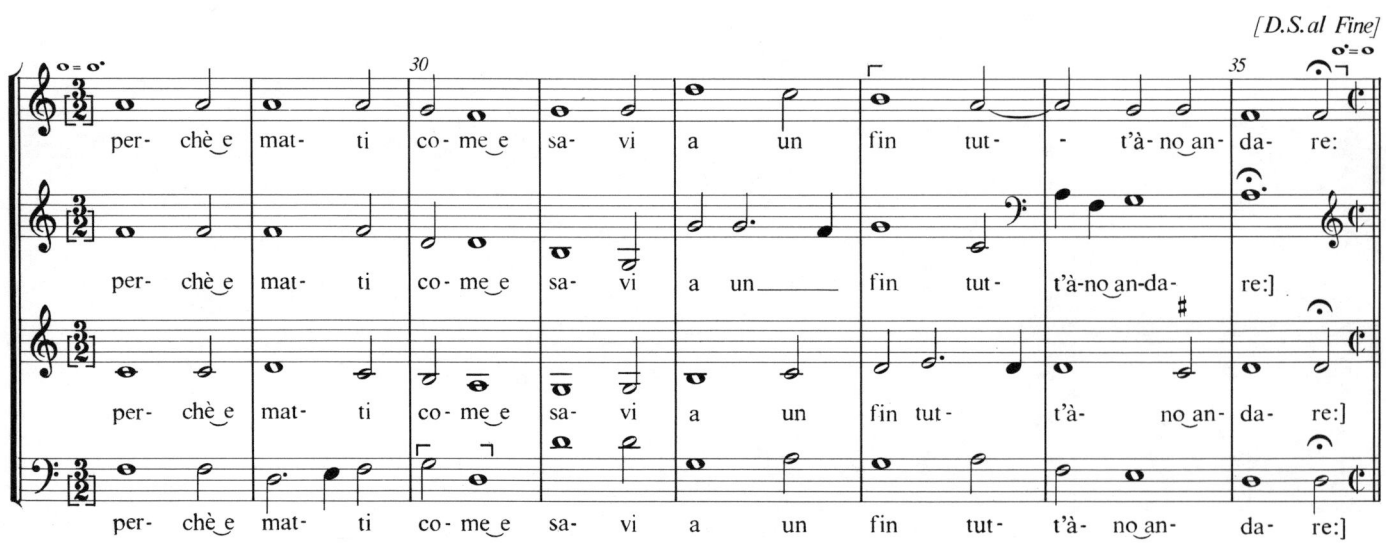

Sanza tanto antivedere
nostra vita a caso fia;
de' sollazi et del godere
seguirèn sempre la via,
che ci par somma pazia
miglior sorte ricerchare: far buon . . .

No' abbiàn di tòr disposto
lo stidion per nostra insegnia,
chè ci par che 'l fare arrosto
cosa sia stimata de degnia;
et ciaschun fra noi s'ingegnia
questa regola observare: far buon . . .

No' corriàn coll'aste in basso,
come franchi paladini;
ma la bestia a ogni passo
ci fa sotto cento inchini;
nè potendo annoi meschini
ritta più la lancia stare,   far buon . . .

Questi giovani galanti
ch'annoi sempre apresso stanno,
sendo noi pocho abbastanti,
al giostrar lor sodisfanno;
perchè a vechi far non sanno
se non sol bere et mangiare: far buon . . .

Dell'entrare sì fieri in giostra
ci dà el vino talvolta ardire,
po' manchare la forza nostra
sentiàn tutta in sul colpire;
ma di poi che riuscire
non ci può questo giostrare,   far buon . . .

[39.] Canto di zingane

Alex. Coppinus
[Alessandro Coppini]

Di paesi lontani et di stran locho,
lasse, venute siàno appocho appocho,
sol per darvi diletto, festa et giocho,
se carità darete a noi meschine.

Ècci fra noi chi ha buon naturale
in lavorar di mano e 'ngegnio tale
che nessun'altra a noi saria equale;
dunque pietà prendete i' noi meschine.

Buona ventura udir da noi potrete,
se 'l vostro sopra 'l nostro metterete,
la man, dico, leggiadra: intenderete
di vostro corso dal principio al fine.

Di sonar, di danzar usiàno ognora
con chi vorrà di voi; farènvi ancora
un guocho: "che l'è drento et che l'è fora,"
che suave piacer porge nel fine.

Però, care madonne, aprite porte,
le qual chiuse tenete, strette et forte,
prima che sopravengha in voi la morte,
prender piacer di noi pover' tapine.

[40.] "Guardate al cielo, el ciel creò costei"

La veste et la corona in fronte mostra
l'erbe, le piante et regni:
ove è el principio della morte vostra.
Di qui nascono e gaudii e pianti et sdegni
delle turbe mortale.
Et lei par che c'insegni
che quel che segue el ben non può aver male.

Primavera, autunno, state et verno,
queste voltavi l' rote.
Mostrono el carro del solar governo
e corivanti armati et seggie vòte.
Sangue, peste et battaglie
l'universo perquote.
Nè può d'alto cadere quel che non saglie.

A te, fanciullo amato da costei,
dimostra frutti et fiori,
che Phebo toglie et dà sopra di lei;
et questi fèr leon, gl'agricultori,
e divin sacerdoti,
a templi expositori
di sancte legge, sacrificii et vòti.

Così, diversi fin, diversi effetti.
Vane et contrarie cose
par che la terra crear si diletti:
ma quanto più suo' secreti nascose
dobbiàn cercar sapere,
perchè tutte le cose
si bramon più che è difficile avere.

Hor questa moltitudin de' viventi
che gli giron dintorno
saran di vita in breve tenpo spenti.
Ma nuove gente ci faran ritorno:
così principio et fine
verrà di giorno in giorno
sinchè 'l ciel s'empierà d'alme divine.

[41.] Canto di lanzi pellegrini

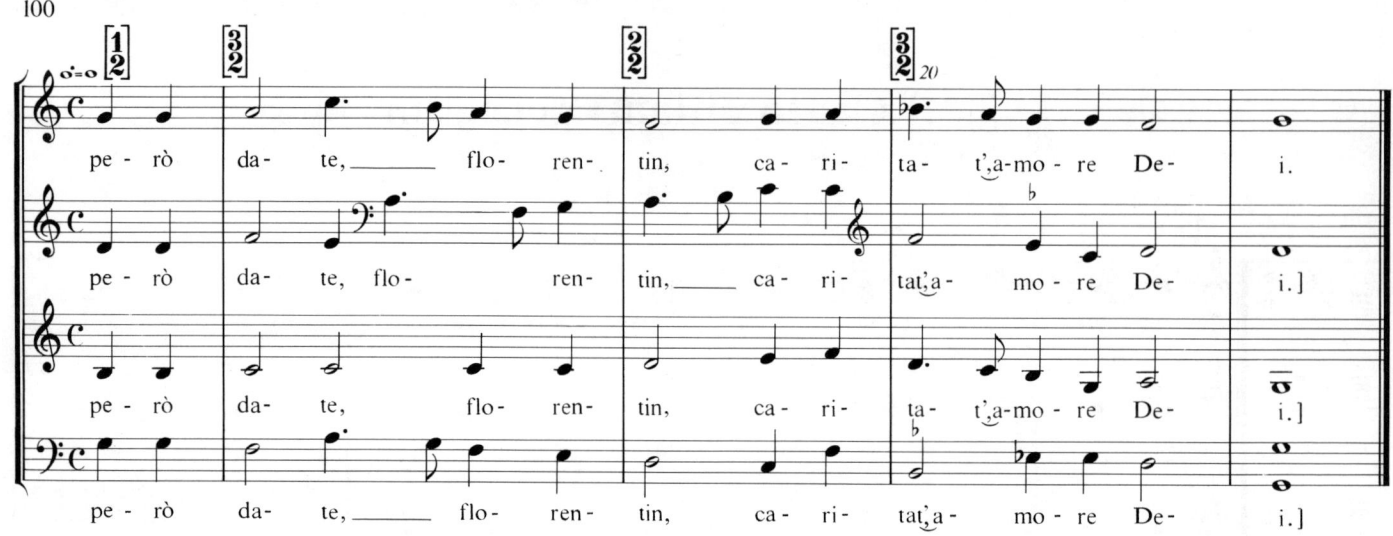

Nelle terre di marchese
gran pericolo à portate
perchè tutte suo paese
star di fangho brodolate:
et però messer, donate
caritate, amore Dei.

Noi afeme in Rome sancte
Cholise e' tutt fetut,
e 'ndulgentie tutte quante
a noi state concedute:
or che star perdon conplute,
caritate, amore Dei.

Queste pofer farlinghotte
punt argent non afer,
star diserto et mal condotte,
nè più sa che sie tener:
però dà, bone messer,
caritate, amore Dei.

Non sapeme bem le vie,
le chamaldoli cerchiàne,
chè là star bon osterie
dalle porte a San Frignane:
date a noi, bone cristiane,
caritate, amore Dei.

[42.] Canto di lanzi sonatori di rubechine

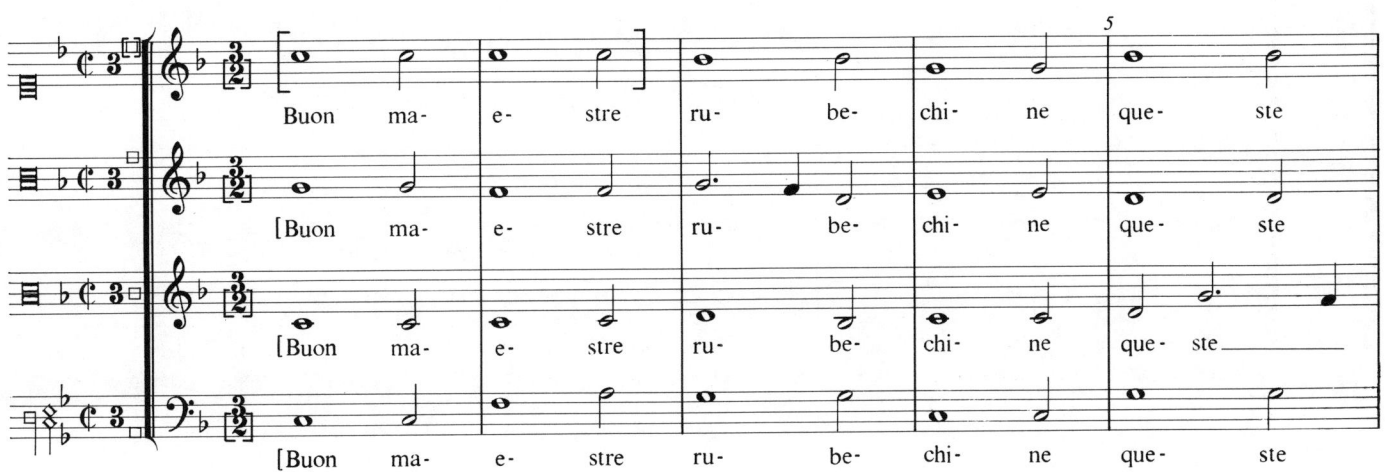

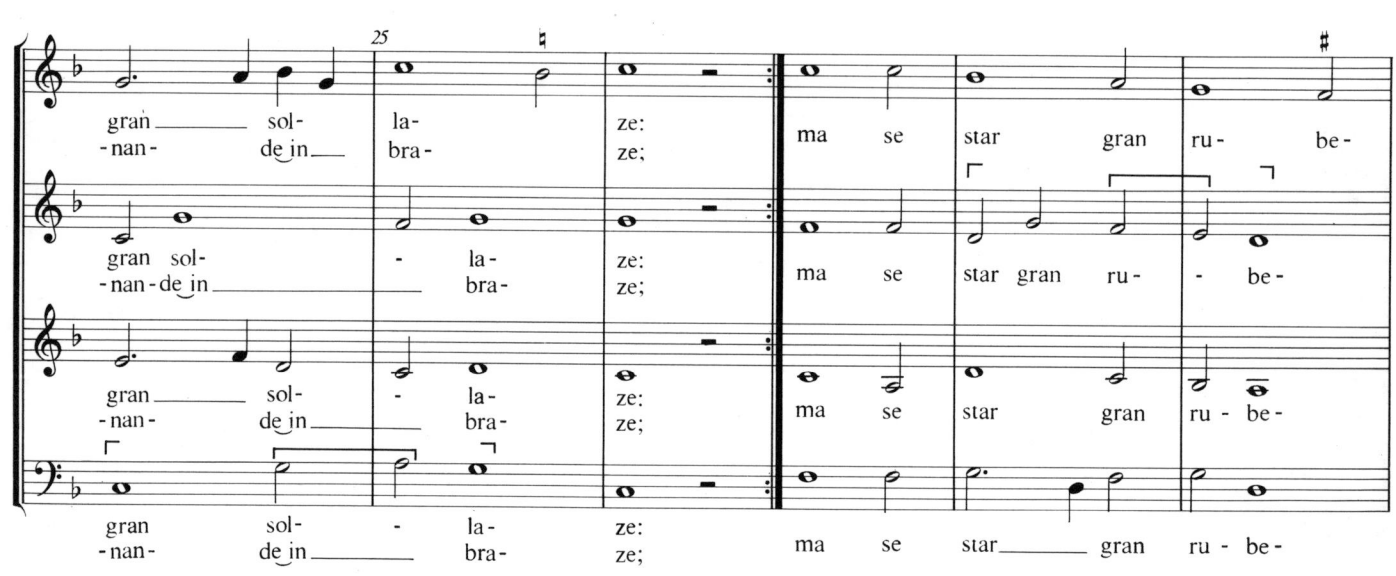

Per pigliar dolce conforte
habbiàn qui nostre marite,
et sonande forte forte,
sappiàn far belle stanpite:
non afer ma' più sentite
sì ghalante coselline.

Per far suone chiare et belle,
quando star corde allentate,
toche queste bischerelle
che qui drente star fichate:
quando afer ben tenperate,
ti far voce ghalantine.

Quando è poi cordate bene,
caze in pugne quest'archette;
sù et giù diguaze et mene,
taste destre et toche nette:
chi più ingegne drente mette
più dolceze sente infine.

Tutte sempre in ogni loche
lanzi star liete et galante,
et con gaudio, festa et guoche
salte, suone, balle et cante:
chè 'l ben nostre tutte quante
stare in queste cotaline.

Se foler con queste suone
far cibatte et bel morescha,
star maestre tutte buone
queste lanzi et noi todesche:
suone ancor quel danz ussesche
che si chiama ciascherine.

[43.] Canto di lanzi venturieri

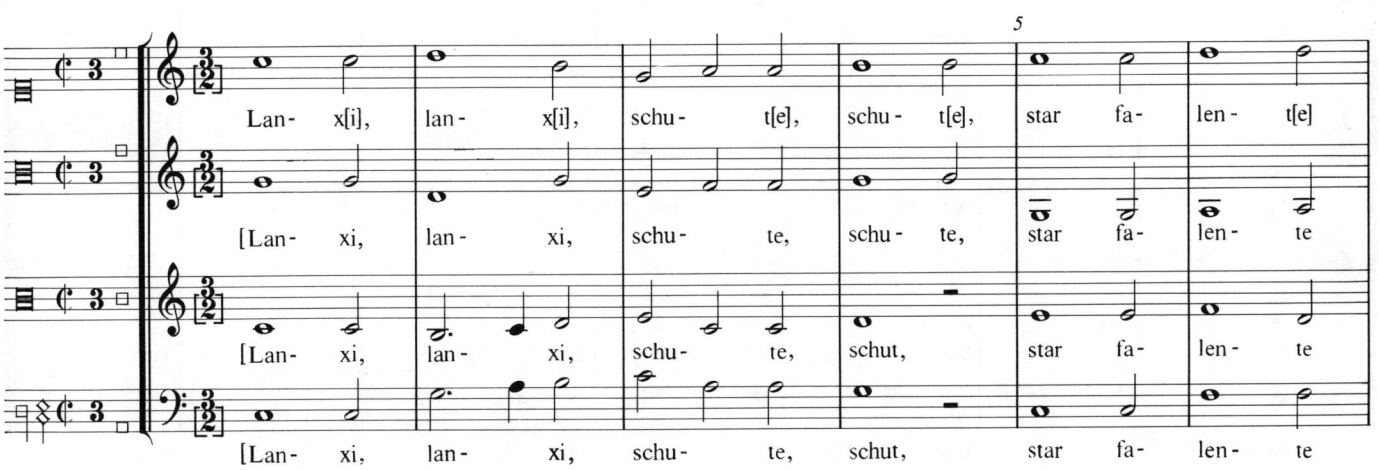

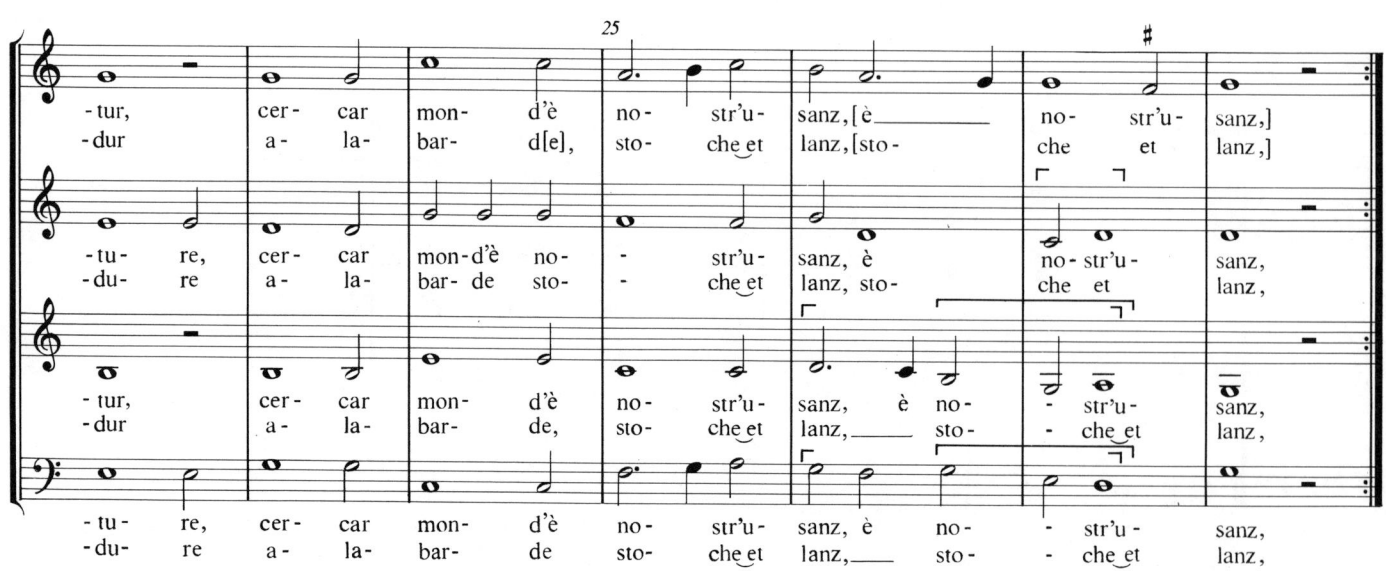

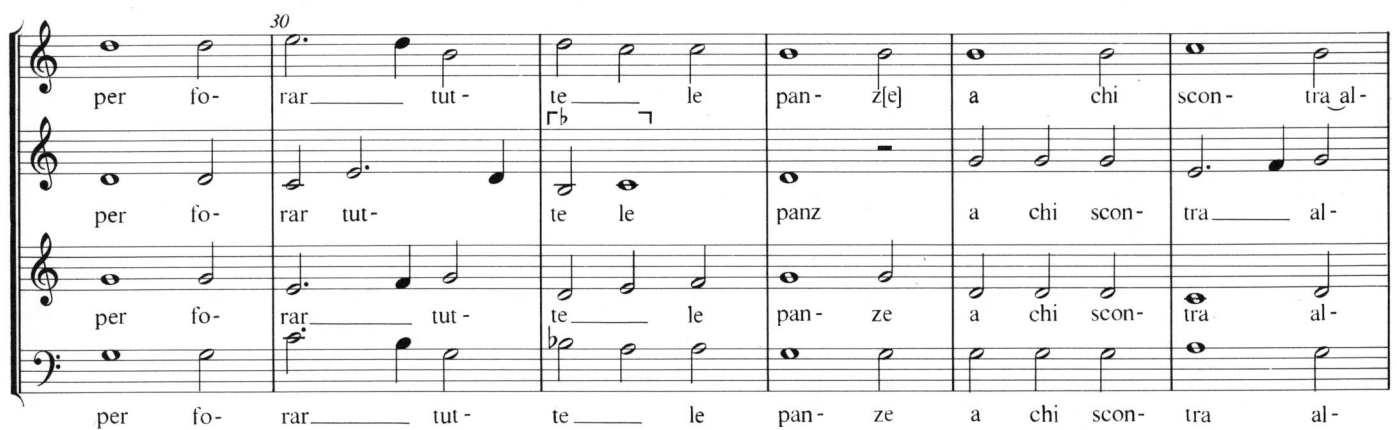

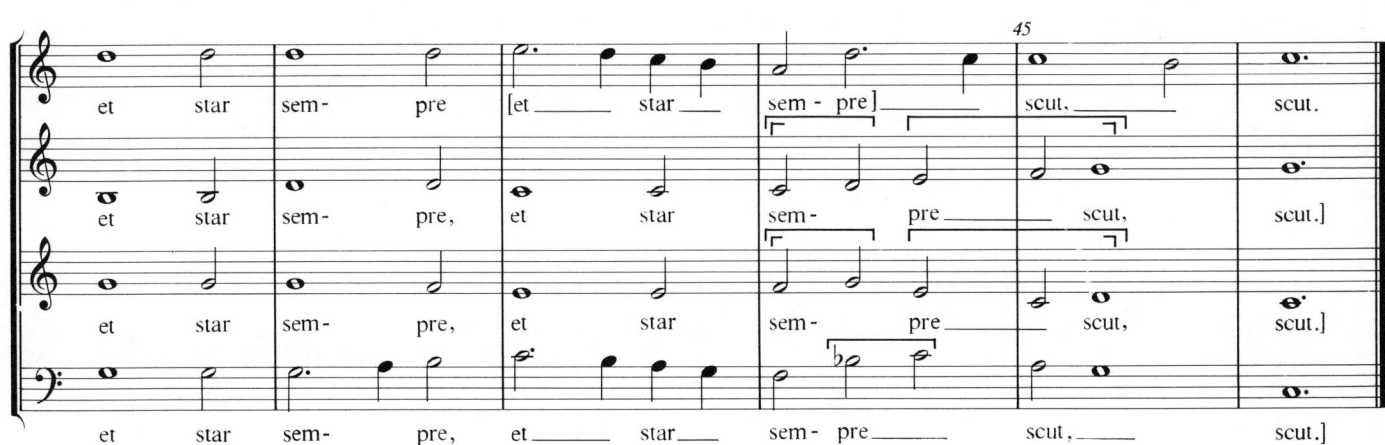

Quando sente tiche tache,
grida lans stroche, stroche,
perchè tutte fuole a sache
metter sempre borghe et roche,
rompe et spexe et far gran fioche,
sparge sangue folentier   ch'a far . . .

Chi parar prochiere o targhe,
lans fort spinze et frughe
tal che prest im piaze larghe
fa parer le strette rughe;
tutta rotta caze in fughe
come diafole et fersiere,   ch'a far . . .

No' star tutte in punte bene
per far fatti allegre et liete;
ma chi fuze et folte stiene,
lanz star poche discrete,
ch'affichar lo stoche driete
mette tutte suo poter: ch'a far . . .